ScribeLife Series

Rooted & Established
In Love

The Power &
Purpose of
*The Greatest
Commandment*

Tonia Woolever

ScribeLife Series

Rooted & Established in Love: The Power & Purpose of the Greatest Commandment

Copyright©2011 Tonia Woolever

ISBN 978-0-9725944-6-2

Published by ScribeLife Publications, 280 Son Shine Circle, Azle, TX 76020, Publishing Division of Shammah Ministries.

Unless otherwise noted, scriptures are quoted from the Holy Bible, New International Version © 1973, 1978, 1984 International Bible Society. Used by permission of Zondervan Bible Publishers.

Scripture quotations marked AMPLIFIED are taken from The Amplified Bible, Old Testament ©1965, 1987 by the Zondervan Corporation. The Amplified New Testament © 1958, 1987 by The Lockman Foundation. Used by permission.

Acknowledgements

I deeply appreciate and happily acknowledge the help of colleagues, family and friends in the preparation of this first book in the ScribeLife Series.

Special thanks to Jody Richards, Nancy Smith, my husband Ron and daughter Gabriele. Your valuable time spent proofreading and offering creative feedback on content, formatting and cover design have made this book better in every way.

I regularly benefit from the strengthening prayers of some wonderful people who love me, love the Lord and love His people. Thank you all for being faithful in your labor of prayer so I could be faithful in my given task.

I love how the Father does Team Kingdom! It is a joy to know the Lord with you all, and see Him more clearly because we are together.

Table of Contents

Why I Write 6

The Greatest Commandment 9

God's Unfailing Love 17

Roots - The Source of Life 23

The Root of Neediness 29

The Root of Fear 35

The Root of Ambition 45

The Root of Law 53

My Introduction To The Love of God 61

One-Sided Love Isn't His Plan 71

First Steps To Being Established In Love 77

Why Is Loving God So Hard For Us? 87

Why Love Is The Greatest Commandment 93

How Do I Love God Like This? 109

You Know You Really Love God When: 121

Conclusion and Prayer 123

More Resources from Shammah Ministries 127

About the Author 129

Why I Write

A. W. Tozer wrote to relieve an unbearable burden of the heart, a burden fueled by what he called "the languishing church around me." I write for much the same reason. I've seen too many for whom Christianity-as-usual has become the emperor who has no clothes, or something they sustain with much effort, like the old showman running madly from one pole to another spinning his plates: "Keep your faith up! Memorize scripture! Confess only success! Never miss church! Give more!" — plus the perpetual struggle to work themselves over in character and habits. A noble effort, successful for some strong-willed souls, but never for me.

I came to God reluctantly, when the pain of a failed life overtook my fear of becoming one of those joyless religious people loaded with rules and no freedom to enjoy life. When a Christian befriended me and kept saying, "Jesus loves you," I began to consider God, though not because I felt like a sinner who needed to be saved. My motives were purely selfish: I craved a satisfying, nurtured life, and a hero upon whose shoulder I could rest my head.

However, I refused to talk myself into believing God loved me. One day I shook my fist at Him and said, "If you're really real, then make me feel your love." Amazingly, He answered my challenge in an unmistakeable, intensely personal way. I had found my hero, and I rested my weary heart on that shoulder.

As a new Christian, John's gospel captivated me with promises of abundant life and personally knowing God's voice. The Psalms and authors like A.W. Tozer, J.I. Packer and John Piper confirmed my initial impression that knowing God intimately was available to all Christians, not just a super-spiritual few, and that one should experience deep pleasure in knowing God.

At times, I didn't know how to know this invisible God, but always ran to Him in my helplessness, not away, and he always met me in my weakness. Again and again it was confirmed that this God carried me, I did not have to carry Him!

Looking back, it is clear that the transformation of my life and character had little to do with strength of will, for I am as weak as they come. Three decades of this Christian pilgrimage have left no doubt that every change has been the inevitable fruit of a life shared with God. My one job has been to believe in his amazing offer of intimacy, extended to every child who comes through Christ to call Him Father.

Furthermore, over 25 years as a pastor's wife, counselor and mentor have given me a front row seat to the lives of believers in every flavor of Christianity, enough to know that the scarcity of transformed, satisfied, joyful disciples of Christ knows no ideological or denominational boundaries. I want to change that. I want convince others that I'm no one special, that we all can find ourselves somewhere in the middle of God's covenant promise that *"They will all know me, from the least of them to the greatest."* I'm looking for the audience who longs to connect with the God I've come to know, to those still living a beggarly Christian life that is unsatisfying and burdensome.

I don't communicate from a platform of success, but from the trenches of life where God has hunkered down with me, when I didn't know how to love my husband, when I couldn't quit smoking, when people broke my heart, when the consequences of my old sins came knocking. I want to reveal the delightful God I've come to know, to help others build their own unique, satisfying life with Him, a life he aptly calls "entering rest."

I wrote this little book as the first in a series to help you find your own life with the one who loves you with an unfailing love, and who deserves to be loved with your whole being. I hope to share with others what I have learned of the workings — and the unmatched joy — of the great and holy labor of love in building the Kingdom of God in the heart of a believer.

Tonia Woolever
December, 2011
Azle, Texas

The Greatest Commandment

"Of all the commandments, which is the most important?"

"The most important one," answered Jesus," is this: ... Love the Lord your God with all your heart and with all your soul and with all your mind and with all your strength." [Mark 12:28-30]

It was an expert in religious law who asked Jesus this question in order to test him. The answer pleased the Pharisee, who — in typical teacher fashion — then taught into the answer Jesus had given:

"To love him with all your heart, with all your understanding and with all your strength...is more important than all burnt offerings and sacrifices." [verses 32-33]

From the time of Moses, burnt offerings and sacrifices had been God's absolute requirements for anyone who wanted to approach Him for worship, to offer thanks, or to make atonement for sin. Jesus and the Pharisee agreed that nothing in all of their religious duties was as important as loving God with one's whole being.

In my early Bible study it surprised me that this command and its twin ("love your neighbor as yourself") are not even listed in the Ten Commandments, yet Jesus said they are the greatest of all. I later learned that like all Jewish men of his day,

Jesus had memorized these words from the time he was first able to learn the Torah, and quoted these scriptures every day from the scroll, which we know today as Deuteronomy 6:4-5. Every Jewish male grew up reciting these words daily.

So here we have it, the nutshell answer to our highest calling as a Christian: love God with all one's heart, with all one's soul, with all one's mind, with all one's strength. And we have here the most important answer to God's open book test, and there WILL be a test on that day. I think it will go something like this: "During your life on earth, when God lived in you (by his Holy Spirit), did you try to love God with every part of who you are?"

Did you try to make choices that would validate your love for God?

Was your behavior more often governed by your love for Him than trying to please yourself or others?

Did you attempt to honor the command to love God in the private thoughts and judgments of your mind?

These are just a few examples of what it means to love God with all one's being.

The salvation of Christ from the curse of original sin has set you free from death and hell. It is an incredible gift from God that enables you to enjoy an even more incredible gift: to become God's own child, grafted into his family, able to know Him as a Father. It's your gift to receive, to embrace, to steward faithfully.

In this transaction you have moved from being a slave to sin to being a beloved, accepted child of God. Therefore, when your body dies in this world and you face your Father in heaven, you will not be judged against a list of rules or mere standards about good and evil; you will be examined as the son or daughter of a Father who gave you everything as an act of love and grace. Any sin you commit as a child of God is now a sin against that relationship, and never more to be measured by the standards of the world.

It's an open book test

Based on Mark 12:28-33, you can be sure you will be judged against the two issues of love: how well did you love God, and how well did you love others. It is an open book test, because we have been provided the answer ahead of that moment.

I believe we will not only face God the Father and God the Son in that moment, but also everyone who shared life with us for even the briefest moment. That is my take on what the greatest command and its twin really mean. Christianity has always been — and will always be — about the relationship, not one's performance against a list of rules.

> *We'll be judged on the two issues of love: how well did you love God, and how well did you love others?*

Did you know that the Apostle Paul pronounced a curse on all those who do not love Jesus? He said this in 1 Corinthians 16:22:

> *"A curse be upon all those who do not love the Lord Jesus Christ."*

Considering how much we currently understand about discovering, removing and avoiding curses, I'm amazed that I've never once heard this one mentioned in a sermon, seminar, book or prayer. In any case, if the proverb is true that says an undeserved curse cannot affect us [Proverbs 26:2], we have nothing to worry about.

Christianity is a relationship, not a set of laws.

From the time of Moses, the Hebrew people were conflicted about God's motives. They said yes to the covenant God offered to them, committing to obey his commandments, while failing to understand that those commands pointed past their obedience to the heart of God. Those commands revealed the way to enjoy nourishing, unbroken life with God and others. His commands — then and now — aren't just rules, they are the elements of great relationship, meant to serve and define a privileged relationship.

But we learn from the Hebrew religious leaders what it looks like to have a heart to honor God while still not having a heart to know and enjoy God. They revealed this motive when they took the original ten commandments and expanded them into hundreds of rules, until the Pharisees of Jesus' day studied, taught and practiced over 600 Jewish laws. They had rules upon rules, and more rules on how to follow those rules. They were burdened with trying to follow all these rules, and laid the same burden upon all those they taught. Their tradition developed into an intense focus on the rules, rather than upon the relationship those rules were intended to enrich. They walked right past the heart of God in their zeal to obey his words to the nth degree!

How did the Hebrews get it so wrong?

Moses begged the Israelites to love God with all their might, and to believe in God's love for them, but they could not. One reason for this is that they were focused on getting from God what they wanted — the "rewards" of following his rules — rather than on enjoying the privilege of having God himself live in their midst. A mindset like that caused them to conclude — when God didn't do things their way — that he did not really love them or have their best interest at heart, and worse: that he could not be trusted.

How did the Hebrew people get it so wrong about God, even after his amazing display of power in delivering them from Egypt? Perhaps it is because they were always staring into their empty plates; they weren't looking for God, they were looking for food. They came out of Egypt laden with treasure and the hope of a new life as free men, but somehow it escaped them that they were being offered the most incredible treasure of all: an exclusive relationship with the creator of the universe. Perhaps they didn't recognize it because this wasn't what they were hungry for.

One of the most heartbreaking scenes in the Bible is found in Numbers 14, where — after the Hebrew spies checked out the Promised Land and found it full of gigantic fruit and giant people — they accused God of evil motives: "Why is the Lord bringing us to this land only to let us fall by the sword?" Their faulty view of God's character prevented the full realization of his unfailing love, a love which became, in effect, wasted on them. The result was that God had to settle for a lesser expression of that love — to bless them as much as possible in the wilderness instead of the Promised Land.

We're still not getting it.

Sadly, this still goes on today in the Body of Christ, and it is producing the same results it did in Jesus' day: people who long to taste the goodness of God end up going away hungry; some grow fat with wealth peddling the favor and blessings of God to those who want a formula for Christian success; too many people redeemed by the blood of Jesus are still largely unchanged in character, and unsatisfied in knowing God. In fact, too many don't know God at all; they have his name and a key to his house but never give themselves permission to go in and enjoy his love — a permission God has freely given. As a result, the life Jesus suffered to give us is not realized — that life of knowing and enjoying the Father in unbroken fellowship.

Again, note that in Jesus' day the Pharisees recited what Christians know now as "The Greatest Command" every day of their lives. Surely this is one of the reasons Jesus was continually frustrated with them, for in spite of knowing these words by heart, having them posted on their door frames, hidden in little boxes they wore on their foreheads, and attached to their arms! — they were experts at looking past God himself while "loving Him" only by intently focusing on all the laws God had given Moses. They taught their disciples to do the same.

As with any habitual daily exercise, they were no doubt numbed to the impact of those words, but Jesus was not. Those words caused him to focus on loving the person that God is, so much that it motivated everything he did, said, chose and believed. He lived the love life, and knew that if he had to choose between love and law, love always trumped the law. As we will see, this motivation is what sustained him all the way to the cross, and helped him endure the death to self that gave birth to our hope of eternal life with God.

The bookends of love

In all of his teaching, miracles and personal examples, Jesus consistently revealed that God's creation is being invited to enjoy the unfailing love of God and to live a life abiding in that love. In return, his creation is asked to love God similarly, in an unfailing way, making all of life's choices with that goal in view. For God and his creation, being loved and loving are the main issues which encompass and define all others. These are the bookends between which one was meant to live life in God's kingdom.

> **Jesus consistently revealed that God's creation is being invited to enjoy the unfailing love of God and to live a life abiding in that love.**

Of all the reasons why some in the Body of Christ have not entered into this life, chief among them is that many have never really experienced the depths of God's love in a personal way. Apart from some marvelous work of the Holy Spirit, most are truly only able to love another when that has been modeled for them, when they have known it firsthand. A true and personal taste of God is promised and encouraged throughout the Scriptures, including the words David penned, *"Taste and see that the Lord is good...."* [Psalms 34:8]

In all the ways that people fail to love God — blindness, hardness of heart, evil inclination or captivity to sin — the only thing which I've seen cure them all is a personal taste of his goodness. I know this was true for me.

There is a reason why the Apostle John said, *We love because he first loved us.* [1 John 4:19] I believe that many — if not all — of those who seem unable to love God, who have little hunger for Him in spite of their salvation, have never personally experienced the depths of God's love. Too many have settled for believing that what little they have felt is as good as it's going to get this side of heaven.

Like the Hebrews of old, many have heard or read of God's personal expressions of love to those still in the land of the living, while not having true faith in it being something they can enjoy. A.W. Tozer wrote in <u>The Pursuit of God</u>:

> *"...for millions of Christians, nevertheless, God is no more real than he is to the non-Christian. They go through life trying to love an ideal and be loyal to a mere principle."*

> *"Over against all this cloudy vagueness stands the clear scriptural doctrine that God can be known in personal experience. A loving Personality dominates the Bible, walking among the trees of the garden and breathing fragrance over every scene. Always a living person is present, speaking, pleading, loving, working, and manifesting Himself whenever and wherever His people have the receptivity necessary to receive the manifestation."* [1]

Tozer spoke from his many years of experience as a pastor and Bible scholar.

Why does the experience of God vary so much from one person to another? I think Tozer's comment shines some light on why some do not experience the depths of God's love: *receptivity*.

We can be sure that God's love is not measured out differently to his various children, so to understand where the problem lies in experiencing that love, we need to look at our end of the matter. The Apostle Paul speaks of God's immeasurable love and gives us huge clues about why we may fail to experience it, all in one fabulous prayer he wrote to the Ephesian Christians.

---

[1] Page 50 The Pursuit of God, A.W. Tozer, Wing Spread Publishers, 2006

God's Unfailing Love

Paul's prayer in Ephesians 3:17-19

Paul burst into prayer occasionally in his letters, and one he wrote in Ephesians absolutely changed my life:

> *May Christ through your faith actually dwell – settle down, abide, make his permanent home – in your hearts! May you be rooted deep in love and founded securely on love, that you may have the power and be strong to apprehend and grasp with all the saints (God's devoted people), the experience of that love, what is the breadth and length and height and depth of it; that you may really come to know – practically, through experience for yourselves – the love of Christ, which far surpasses mere knowledge without experience; that you may be filled through all your being unto all the fullness of God – that is, may have the richest measure of the divine presence, and become a body wholly filled and flooded with God himself.* [Amplified]

One of the most profound prayers in the New Testament, it teaches us much. Consider the elements of Paul's prayer:

- That your faith would result in God (the Holy Spirit) making his permanent home in your heart.

- That you would be deeply rooted and securely established in God's love.

- That you would have the power and strength necessary to perceive and experience — i.e., be receptive to — the incredible dimensions of the love of Christ.

- That experiencing this love is far superior to just having knowledge about it.

- That the goal and result of experiencing God's love is to have the fullest possible measure of his Divine presence.

This removes salvation far away from being a mere "get out of hell free" card. If you take Paul's prayer at face value, it should ruin your ability to settle for less. Because you, like every other mortal, crave to be loved like this. Proverbs 19:22 recognizes this truth when it says, What a man desires is unfailing love.

We keep trying to satisfy our love hunger elsewhere

I don't care who you are: man, woman, old or young, scholar, soldier, CEO or housewife, you were created to thrive in a relationship of unfailing love. The only reason we search for anything else to satisfy our souls is that we fear we will never find this unfailing love. We are afraid to hope that it really exists, or even if it does, that someone would think enough of us or be good enough to love us like this.

Therefore, when people fail to love us as they should, our fears are confirmed, and we are wounded. As a result, we learn to look elsewhere for something to satisfy us. We may be able to quiet that hunger temporarily, and if so, an appetite develops for that thing or person which has helped us forget our great need to be deeply loved.

In the same way that we develop addictions for sugar or other junk foods that one's body does not truly need for life, we also develop a hunger for things that not only fail to give us life, they rob us of it in the long run. They can actually starve us and bring us to crippling dependence upon drugs, foods, people, ambitions. These acquired tastes are established in us every time we reach for something other than the life which our Creator God offers.

What we give our hunger to is where we sink our roots.

Like a tree that develops its root system by sending out feeders on the hunt for nourishment, we become rooted in whatever we reach for to satisfy our needy hearts. Many Christians who have been genuinely redeemed, who are on their way to heaven, have never yet become rooted in the unfailing love of God as a basis for their new life. For many it is a lack of proper mentoring or teaching by those who should be discipling them; for others it is a blindness that comes from the need to stay in complete control of their lives; for some it is a lack of faith in what God has said, both about Himself and about us. As a counselor I've seen many people have trouble connecting with God's love when they have been deeply wounded in their relationships with others.

Sometimes I wonder if it would be more productive for church pastors to send everyone home for a season to seek only to know the love of God, rather than continue with our endless church services as usual. Far too many churchgoers are still just going through the motions, showing up more spectators than worshippers.

> **Many Christians have never yet become rooted in the unfailing love of God as a basis for their new life.**

Many simply have not been discipled in the basic steps taught so clearly in the New Testament and so beautifully summarized in Paul's prayer. If experiencing God's love were an automatic slam-dunk for every believer, then the church, the world and you would have a very different quality of life. The devil hates you because God loves you, and I've come to believe that the focus of most of the devil's schemes is to separate you from (actually experiencing) the love of Christ.

Love is not approval

Understand this: being loved by God doesn't mean that God approves of what you do or who you are. To us mortals, love seems invariably connected to approval, adoration, admiration, and the assumption that somehow you deserve to be loved. God's love for you has nothing to do with any of these things. God loves you because he's a lover. God's love isn't based upon how much you satisfy Him, it is based upon his desire to express the best of who he is — and he is love. It is about him and the glory of his being. Simply put, it gives God joy to love you with all his might.

Of course, it is possible to bless God so much that it evokes in Him esteem, approval, adoration or admiration for you. As with any relationship, these things are the natural fruit one reaps from sowing seeds of love and honor; but the fact remains that God's unfailing love for you is something you cannot earn and you cannot make it go away.

The devil will tell you often that you're not worthy of God's love. Quite frankly, this is true; apart from Christ, you are not worthy of God's love— no one is — nonetheless, he loves us! That is the awesome grace of God; it's who He is. *God is love.* [1 John 4:8, 16]

You are loved because of who God is; so your worthiness is not the issue; yet through Jesus Christ you have been made worthy. (God loves all men, but only believers can count on enjoying the blessings of his immeasurable, faithful love.) So the next time the devil whispers in your ear, "You don't deserve to be loved by God," say, "Yes, that's true, but that doesn't stop God from loving me with all his might!"

I am still a very flawed individual, but no longer afraid of my flaws. I do not have to live in fear that my weaknesses will cost me the love, acceptance and companionship of the Lord that I need to walk through this life. In fact, as the years pass I see more and more of the truth of who I am and have been, and so his grace towards me grows more amazing, not less. I have learned that the safest place to see the truth about myself is in the light of God's wonderful love. The shame and sorrow I feel in these times always give way to hope. I have learned to run to God in my shame, not away from Him, because I know his motives toward me. I know from experience that in his love he will change me as I cling to Him in committed love.

However, we mortals aren't good at loving people in spite of their flaws, and we have a nasty tendency to love or withhold love as a form of manipulation. In other words, "I will show you love if you please me." We tend to think that God is the same way, but he is not. His love is steadfast and does not waver with our behavior. In his love, God is motivated to bring forth the best in his beloved. Sometimes that "best" is brought forth through discipline, but Scripture assures us that discipline is a validation of his love, not a punishment for misbehavior.

You can't do anything to make God love you more or to make Him love you less. All you can do is decide if you're going to receive God's love in the way he gives it.

I have chosen to rest in and enjoy God's love. That choice alone made a huge difference in "receptivity," my ability to perceive God's ways of loving me. It's like the saying on a rock in my garden: "Some things have to be believed to be seen."

Back to Paul's prayer in Ephesians: it leaves no doubt that "Job One" for every believer should be to understand what it means to be rooted and established in God's love.

Roots - The Source of Life

> *I pray that out of his glorious riches he may strengthen you with power through his Spirit in your inner being, so that Christ may dwell in your hearts through faith. And I pray that you, being rooted and established in love, may have power, together with all the saints, to grasp how wide and long and high and deep is the love of Christ, and to know this love that surpasses knowledge — that you may be filled to the measure of all the fulness of God. (Ephesians 3:16-19)*

One day as I read these words in Ephesians, I was struck by Paul's phrase, "rooted and established in love." I thought of how Jesus taught that life in the Kingdom is like a grain of a mustard seed, which is the tiniest of seeds, but when planted in good soil becomes one of the largest of all garden plants.

Every gardener knows that a plant flourishes above the soil only when a strong root system has developed below the ground. The unseen root system is, together with sun and rain, the source of life and nourishment. Without this hidden expression of life in the soil, there can be no enduring vitality, and the plant will eventually wither and die. In fact, without a healthy root system the sun and rain meant to feed the plant would actually overwhelm it.

Look at Paul's prayer again, and notice that Paul speaks as if he assumes his listeners had already been rooted and established in God's love. I think perhaps in those first years of the Church, such an experience was much more common; a theory supported by the legendary passion, power, commitment and fruitfulness of those firstfruits believers, those ordinary people that turned into world-changers. They didn't get that way because they took a seminar, or because they were perfectionists. Paul had been one of those and it had never produced the life in him that his heart-to-heart encounter with Christ did. So when Paul speaks, I listen.

Roots

When a tree is newly established in soil, its first job is to send down a taproot. The taproot is the main one that goes straight down, whose job is to anchor the tree, so that together with the lateral roots which begin to develop, the tree can stand upright. If the tree cannot stand strongly upright, any fruit that develops will put such a strain on it that the fruit itself may contribute to the tree's fall, even perhaps its death.

During the first year or two the main root system gradually becomes a wide-spreading root system with numerous horizontal-growing surface roots and a few vertical, deep-anchoring roots. This aggressive network of lateral roots spreads out from the tree like spokes on a wheel after the taproot is established.

What causes these roots to develop? They grow day by day as a result of searching for nourishment in the soil.

The taproot remains the most vital root, so that even if no rain falls for a long time, the tree can still take moisture from deep within the earth. And if that taproot finds a hidden spring of water, the tree will never thirst, no matter how dry the conditions above ground become. In fact, this is the secret of trees planted alongside a river or stream, who are watered constantly. David compared the blessed man or woman of God to such a tree:

> **Roots grow day by day as a result of searching for nourishment.**

> *He is like a tree planted by streams of water, which yields its fruit in season and whose leaf does not wither. Whatever he does prospers. (Psalm 1:3)*

Again, the most important point of this illustration is the fact that what causes a root to grow is the act of seeking nourishment; every root grows stronger as it reaches out into the soil to find food. Roots inevitably develop wherever we reach for that which sustains life; where they grow reveals where you've gone hunting for nourishment.

By now you've guessed my point: that the soil of God's love is the only place to grow a healthy Christian. Your faith in God's love — demonstrated by reaching for God, trusting in Him and his Word — leads to the growth of that taproot in your first years as a Christian. When Paul speaks of having been rooted and established in God's love, this is, in part, what he means. Being strongly rooted in that love provides the anchor that holds you through every storm and every drought as your relationship to God goes through season after season. It is what anchors you while you develop those lateral roots of human relationships in the Body of Christ — a subject for a later book in this series. You were created to thrive through the unfailing love of God.

Aimed at the wrong target

Here's the problem: most of the teaching in churches today is focused on your duty to be conformed to the likeness of Christ, which at first glance seems right on. Typically you will hear more sermons on how to be a good Christian than you will on being loved by God. In this we have gotten the cart before the horse.

You see, the ability to be a good Christian, to take on the likeness of Christ, happens most naturally as you personally experience the love of the Lord. You were meant to become like Him, not by making yourself follow rules, but as a direct result (or fruit) of experiencing God's love — just like children become like their parents because they share life for years.

As John the Apostle said, we are able to love like Christ only because we have first been loved by Christ. Becoming like Him happens organically, naturally as you experience His love personally. You may still get there by working hard to make yourself change, but it is typically harder — and there are usually more "dropouts" this way because leaning into God's love gives rise to joy, and apart from intimacy with Christ you may never get to the joy. Without joy your life as a Christian can be reduced to an act of will-power and become a drudge.

If being rooted and established in love is "Job One" as a Christian, you need to examine your life with God and ask, am I there? Is this what I have, or what I am developing? And if I am not being rooted in God's love, then what is my relationship to God rooted in?

Teaching tools are great to strengthen you as long as they truly draw you near to God and do not carry you off into a devotional life stuffed with everything but simple fellowship with the Lord Himself. Too often we seek after more and more of these things when we don't feel close enough to God, when the thing we need most is to go to a quiet place and call his name, and set our desire upon Him. There is a veritable buffet of Christian material out there, and I too have stuffed myself on it at times, only to discover later that I'm still not satisfied. It all tastes good, looks good, feels good for awhile, but none of it satisfies like a quiet half-hour alone with the Lord, hearing his voice, feeling his love, receiving his personal instruction.

Jesus addressed our tendency to reach for our favorite props instead of God Himself when he said to the Pharisees:

> *You diligently study the Scriptures because you think that by them you possess eternal life. These are the Scriptures that testify about me, yet you refuse to come to me to have life. (John 5:39–40)*

By all means, read your Bible, every word of it. God will meet you in it and through it, build a platform in you from which you can learn to know Him and hear His voice. But even Bible reading was never meant to be a substitute for face-to-face relationship with the Living God. Remember, those who paved the way for us to know God had no Bibles to study. Noah, Abraham, Moses, Joshua, David and others primarily knew God by communion with His Spirit. Read the Word, but go to Jesus Christ daily to find your life. Is it not written,

> **Nothing satisfies like a quiet half-hour alone with the Lord, hearing his voice, feeling his love, receiving his personal instruction.**

For you died, and your life is now hidden with Christ in God. (Colossians 3:3)

What we're really hungry for is what we go after.

What we really hunger for motivates all we do. It determines where we set our souls to graze for nourishment. It leads us to the choices we make about how we spend our time, our money, our attention. We instinctively reach for anything which satisfies our immediate needs, whatever makes life feel abundant or good or safe or even just manageable. What we reach for becomes the soil that we sink our roots into.

What are you rooted in?

You need to know what you are rooted in in order to understand why you are thriving, or failing to thrive, in knowing God. The root is the very basis of your relationship to God, the place where you hold onto God. What forms this foundation in your soul and spirit? Under what (heart) condition was your relationship to God established? Unfortunately, many Christians are rooted in something other than God's love, having had their relationship to Him established through some other goal, however unintentional.

To know what you are rooted in, look to your hunger. What you long for, what you believe you need, becomes the motive for all that you do, all that you reach for. What you consistently seek to satisfy your hunger with determines what you become. It is true that "you are what you eat." In the next sections we will look at some common — and flawed — roots of relationship. I hope you don't find yourself there, but if you do, be encouraged, there is a remedy: it is never too late to sink your roots down into God's love.

The Root of Neediness

Were you originally drawn to God in hopes of having your needs met, either materially through the charity of a local church, or through a Christian TV personality offering to help you "appropriate the blessings" of God? If so, you might be rooted in neediness.

The truth is that we are all needy, and our need should drive us to God. Nonetheless, neediness is not a healthy foundation for a relationship — as countless people in unsatisfying co-dependent marriages can verify. Such relationships inevitably end up being measured against a list of needs rather than the joy and fulfillment of sharing life.

If your relationship to God is rooted in neediness, your primary motivation in connecting with God is to get your needs met, your blessings claimed, your prosperity ensured. You are in danger of becoming a user of God, rather than a lover of God. Furthermore, whatever motivates you inevitably shapes how you relate to others.

Judas is a good example of one who was rooted in neediness. He helped himself to the purse whenever he wanted, because he was more concerned with his need than with Jesus' mission. His need for material provision caused him to become a thief, and his political agenda caused him to sell Jesus out.

Your relationship to God may be rooted in neediness if:

1. You drift away from God when he doesn't give you what you want. In such instances your faith in God

wavers easily, you lose heart for the relationship, and your devotion grows cold.

2. Your thanksgiving and praise fall silent when God has not come through as you believe He should, and gratitude is replaced with disappointment or anger. It's very hard to sing songs of praise in church or read your Bible. Bitter feelings may creep in.

3. You are diligent to pray about your "needs" list, but never drawn to prayer just to enjoy God's presence or spend time with Him just to know Him more. When life is humming along good you have little motivation to pray. Or prayer may just be something you force yourself to do because it's right.

Truly, God wants to meet your needs; in fact, he abundantly meets the needs of his children! But God should not be used; as a parent it probably feels the same to Him as it does to us. As a parent I experienced being used by my children when they went through the self-absorbed seasons of childhood. While I know they have always loved me, in their immature days they were capable of trying to manipulate me to get what they wanted. It is also easy to look back on my childhood and recognize times when I treated my own parents this way.

Most parents naturally desire to provide for their children without accounting as to whether they will get anything in return. But as the child grows up a parent does begin to expect something, and that is to be treated as someone valued and enjoyed, not simply as the one who pays the bills and buys the goodies. If this doesn't happen because the child remains focused on his own needs and becomes established in an attitude of entitlement rather than gratitude, the parent will inevitably (and appropriately) feel used. Such a parent will likely still give, but have little joy in it. On the other hand, a child who expresses love and value for the parent — apart from whether the child is given everything they want — increases the parents' joy AND their desire to give!

When you love someone deeply, it creates a hunger in you that is only satisfied by being with them and by freely expressing all your goodness and your strength to them. You want to give yourself to them, and be known by them. God the Father loves you like this.

Bring all your needs to God, but don't be a user.

Like many, I came to the Lord in neediness; I needed someone greater than myself who could help me live life right and become the woman I dreamed of being. I needed someone to pay the price for my sin. It was a while before I knew that I just needed Him, the person that God is, and that in having Him, I have everything I need.

It is right to bring all your needs to God, but there is a vast difference between trusting Christ for all your needs, and being rooted in neediness. It actually honors God for you to go to Him in your neediness, rather than seek to fill it by your own strength.

> **It was a while before I knew that I just needed Him, the person that God is, and that in having Him, I have everything I need.**

The one rooted in neediness is in danger of being a user of God instead of a lover. He may be easily led into greed, especially if he often feeds at the table of those who focus primarily on the prosperity teachings of the Bible. While it is true that God wants to prosper his true Covenant children (read that "faithful ones"), focusing on achieving prosperity more than loving God can lead to a perversion of faith, and establish a new believer in a root of greed instead of love. This ultimately robs God's child of the greatest treasure God has to give: Himself.

So while God's promises of abundance and faithful provision are true, we must not treat God like Santa Claus or presume upon his promises while neglecting his heart. Jesus warned us to be on guard against all kinds of greed [Luke 12:15] and Paul said that among God's holy people there should not be "even the hint" of greed [Ephesians 5:3].

God wants to satisfy his people.

Jesus promised that those who come to God with their neediness will be filled, which is why he called Himself the Bread of Life. However, God would satisfy far more souls if those souls were hungry for the Lord Himself, not just what he gives. King David learned this vital secret, and wrote of the joy of having his soul satisfied by God in Psalm 63:

> "O God, you are my God, earnestly I seek you; my soul thirsts for you, my body longs for you, in a dry and weary land where there is no water. I have seen you in the sanctuary and beheld your power and your glory. Because your love is better than life, my lips will glorify you. I will praise you as long as I live, and in your name I will lift up my hands. My soul will be satisfied as with the richest of foods; with singing lips my mouth will praise you."
> [verses 1-5]

When I think of rich foods, chocolate cheesecake comes to mind, so I think of that when I read David's words. I should expect knowing God to satisfy me every bit as much. I do not diminish God by saying this; I'm simply acknowledging that we mortals love the satisfaction of food, those things we can taste and smell and see and savor. We should expect God's love will be every bit as satisfying to us, in ways just as real, when the heart has a genuine encounter with the Living God that goes beyond simple faith that God is present "up there" somewhere.

David had faith in God's *presence*, and used his faith to draw from Him all that he would expect in relating to a flesh-and-blood person. He said to God, *"Your love is ever before me..."* [Psalm 26:3] which revealed that his eyes were focused on the God who loved him, rather than on his neediness. Author Erich Fromm said in his work "The Art of Loving:"

Immature love says: "I love you because I need you."
Mature love says: "I need you because I love you."

David is a perfect example of one who had all his needs met because he valued the person of God and found satisfaction in sharing life with Him. David wrote from REAL experience with a REAL god in REAL life, and that life took shape without benefit of church conferences, spiritual growth books and CD's, or whiz-bang preachers on TV. He became rooted and established in God's love in the sheepfold, the caverns and the battlefield. He did this only with the same helper we have: the Holy Spirit.

With the Holy Spirit's help David experienced God's presence, was strengthened by God's love in ways that gave him courage and hope. He wrote of this as God's "unfailing covenant love." Don't make the mistake of dismissing David's experience as something only for a special few. You live in the time of the New Covenant of Jesus, by which God promises that "they will all know me, from the least of them to the greatest." [Hebrews 8:10-12]. If you have come to trust Christ as your Savior, you fit in there somewhere; and if you stop making excuses about why you can't know God, and/or stop trusting the doctrines of men more than the simple truth presented in the Bible, you'll find yourself there.

> **God's promise:**
> **"They will all know me, from the least of them to the greatest."**

When God offered Himself in covenant to Abraham, he said, "I AM your shield, your very great reward." The relationship he invited Abraham into was one that offered great promises and provision, but all was meant to flow out of a relationship of mutually committed love and accountability. We who are called "the seed of Abraham" are likewise offered amazing gifts from God, the greatest of which is knowing Him as a Father, with all the privileges that attend being a son or daughter of God. Every Christian is invited into a covenant whose benefits can only be enjoyed through childlike trust and resting in the Holy Spirit's work and power. One of the reasons why "the greatest command" is at the top of God's list is that he knew the best way to give you his life was to insist that you know Him in love.

The Root of Fear

Were you originally drawn to God because you were afraid of going to hell? Do you live with a nagging anxiety that you never really please God? Do you think of Him as some sort of big policeman in the sky?

Although the fear of going to hell is a good reason to come to God, it was never meant to be the foundation or definition of your relationship to a loving Father. If you have not moved beyond whatever fear may have brought you to God, you will always live by the door, on the outside looking in, never feeling like you belong in the arms of God, never relaxing into the full acceptance offered through the atonement of Jesus Christ.

God describes life in covenant with Him as "entering rest," which is exactly what it feels like when you live by faith in his love. But this rest never comes to those rooted in fear towards God.

But, you may ask, doesn't the Bible say we must fear God? Yes, it does. In fact, Isaiah foretold of Jesus that he would "delight in the fear of the Lord." But we need to understand the difference between a right fear and a wrong fear of God.

Two kinds of fear

There is what I call a dreadful fear, and an awesome fear. Dreadful fear causes us to shrink away from God and live in fear of punishment if we mess up — which feels all too easy to do. This kind of fear is an abiding anxiety about the motives of God, and it produces little more than a grudging appeasement of Him who is felt to be a cosmic and distant judge.

> **Dreadful fear is an abiding anxiety about the motives of God.**

For a Christian rooted in dreadful fear, God is always the harsh task master. This dreadful fear motivated the servant who buried his talent in the ground because he assumed his master was too demanding and unfair. In his anxiety (and the wrong assumption that it produced, like "Nothing will please you anyway") — the servant decided it was better to not even try anything rather than risk the wrath of a too-hard-to-please master.

Dreadful fear of God is only appropriate for those who are outside the family of God, who will face his wrath at the end of all things. Those outside of covenant with God should dread Him, for he will destroy all who have rejected his son Jesus at the end of time, who have scoffed at both his sacrificial love and his place as Creator-King. But this is not so for those who have truly come into relationship with God the Father through his son Jesus, who are called to come near to God in the intimacy that flows between a father and his beloved child.

Dreadful fear prevents us from entering into this intimacy, and is completely inappropriate for a covenant child of God who is invited to call God "Father" after placing faith in the atoning blood of Christ.

Awesome fear is very different. While dreadful fear makes you want to go away from God, awesome fear draws you TO God. It increases as you experience more of his majesty and righteousness. Jesus' fear of the Father was not a terror of Him; it was an awesome reverence for Him as the self-existent, omnipotent God, the sovereign ruler over all things, the one who is righteous in every way. Awesome fear should produce the same thing in us that it did in Jesus: an attitude of reverent submission that governs our conduct and leads us to faithful obedience. Love will produce reverent submission in us. Submission is seen as a weakness to some; the very word sends up a red flag in some circles. But Jesus lived a life that said submission is an act of love.

Healthy fear of God is accompanied by the thought, "I love you so much, I can't bear to disappoint you." It is similar to the restraint a child feels at the thought of violating a parent's values or rules and the inevitable consequences — not just the punishment, but the shame that interrupts the free flow of affection and goodness between them. It is a healthy fear of violating an intimate relationship; but in order to arrive at this kind of fear we first have to have the intimate relationship. The fear of losing or damaging that relationship, combined with a desire to honor the beloved, provides motivation to do what is right. This kind of fear is really love by another name.

The one who is rooted in a dreadful fear of God may end up struggling continually with obedience. We see two very different results from these two kinds of fear in the cause-and-effect cycle of relationship.

The Cycle of Fear and Disobedience

In the cycle of fear, we are anxious and unsure of God's motives, or unsure about our ability to know God's will. We are afraid of messing up if we do the wrong thing, so we don't obey Him. Guilt is now added to the anxiety, so we avoid facing God. We have chosen our own [safe] way instead of his, and while our path will continue to be watched over by our faithful God, we will have trouble believing in that fact; plus, this will not be the same as walking WITH God, where the greatest blessings come.

The more we keep going our own way, the more we reinforce our fear of God and the nagging belief that he is unhappy with us. If we keep this up long enough our hearts become hard as our walls of self-protection get bigger. Failing to walk with God, blessings do not attend our way, and we may fall into troubles. Eventually, we may end up shaking our fist at

God, saying "Why did you let this happen?" — or worse, accusing God of evil motives.

We become rooted in fear as a result of being hungry for safety and self-control, and because we do not put faith in God's unfailing love. So the cycle of fear is that we disobey, and in taking our own path instead of obeying God, we open ourselves to bad things. I often say that God doesn't have to come up with a punishment for the disobedience of his children; all he has to do is let us have what we want and our choices will eventually punish us. (Scripture bears this out, by the way.) And if we refuse to see this truth, our hearts grow harder towards God, and our fears are reinforced: God either is not good, or isn't going to be good to me in a way I can enjoy. Why try to obey?

> **We become rooted in fear as a result of being hungry for safety and self-control.**

The Cycle of Love and Obedience

The cycle of love and obedience goes like this: We first hear God loves us, wants to guide us and give us life. We believe. We listen for his commands in prayer, we read them in the Bible. We do what he says, even if it is sometimes a little scary or uncomfortable or requires a sacrifice. As we take the first step in obedience by saying "Yes!" in our hearts, the Spirit comes alongside and to help us carry out our choice. This causes us to experience anew his fellowship, his strength, his love. We come through the experience knowing more than ever that it is true that God loves us; this in turn makes us eager to obey the next time.

This is the cycle of love: we either obey because we love, or because we want to love, and that obedience brings us to a greater experience of God's love. Jesus wrote of this in John 15:9-10:

Now remain in my love. If you obey my commands, you will remain in my love, just as I have obeyed my Father's commands and remain in his love.

When you say yes to God no matter how hard it is on you, the experience of walking with God through that act of obedience causes you to see how wonderful He really is. You see and experience God in a whole new way, that causes you to love Him more!

Fear inspires the need to control.

In fact, fear will make you want to stay in complete control of your relationship with God. Fearful people need to feel safe, and it is only by exercising control over what others do to them that their fear is abated. Those who are rooted in fear often yield to the need to control everything and everyone around them, so they won't have to be afraid of what might happen.

People who are rooted in such fear find surrender to the Lord excruciatingly difficult. They also have trouble hearing God's voice in prayer (or even wanting to hear God's voice) for fear of what he will say or ask of them.

Those who seem to have an easy time obeying God are not necessarily spiritual giants; they are more likely to be ordinary people who have realized that God can be trusted, who are not afraid to abandon themselves completely to his will.

Relating to God as Father and King

Your task as a covenant child of God is to maintain true reverence (awesome fear) for your Creator-King, yet approach Him in confidence that you will always be accepted and that he will be pleased that you have come near. For the children of the King, the role of "Father's child" trumps the role of "King's subject."

We commonly struggle with balancing the reverential fear of God with his invitation to intimacy. It confuses our senses that the one who has power over all creation, over every nation and the universe, invites us to come close and be familiar. But that is the beauty of our heavenly Father and the nature of his heart. To fully embrace both positions is to have a right relationship with Him. Jesus modeled for us the perfect balance of walking in an awesome fear of displeasing the Father and the intimacy to which we are called as his children.

> **God's glory is revealed in relationship.**

It cannot be emphasized enough that Jesus not only saved you from your sin, he made it possible for you to personally know God. This is the explicit promise of the New Covenant of Christ (see Hebrews 8:10-12), and if you read your Bible from cover to cover you cannot escape the fact that God wants to know and be known by his creation. He has paid the ultimate price to make it possible and provided everything you need to do this. What is He after? Building a kingdom, yes, but I believe his purpose in doing that is to reveal his glory, which is his goodness. A huge component of that is God's way of being a father, lover, provider, defender and ruler.

God's glory is revealed in relationship. Because He delights for you to personally taste of this goodness, God invites you to approach Him in childlike trust and presume upon his love and grace. A dreadful fear of God would never permit such presumption. While the fear of the Lord is the beginning of wise relating to God [Proverbs 9:10], love takes you places where fear could never go.

There is a scene in the movie "Anna and The King" that perfectly illustrates the unique access offered to the child of a king. In this story the fierce King of Siam has no trouble executing severe discipline on those who violate the strict protocol of his court, in which no one is allowed to enter his presence, speak to him or even look him in the eye without his permission.

One day while conducting the kingly business of his court, one of the king's tender young sons comes bursting in the room, runs through all the guards, the court officials and the many subjects who are bowed low with eyes to the ground, straight to his father. All court business is forgotten, all subjects dismissed, as the previously stern king scoops his son into his lap and asks with all fatherly tenderness, "What is it, my son?" The moment I saw this I was immediately struck by how it perfectly pictures reality for a Christian.

We have this kind of access to our heavenly Father, to the King of all Kings. If we shrink back in fear that we are nothing more than his unworthy (and therefore unwelcome) subjects, we dishonor the invitation to approach as his beloved children, and we demonstrate a lack of trust in his Word that he will receive us. 1 Peter 3:12 assures us:

> *"For the eyes of the Lord are on the righteous and his ears are attentive to their prayer..."*

Like the son of the King of Siam, our perfection is not to be found in being a perfect subject, but in honoring our Father by running to Him, knowing Him, learning from Him, staying close so we can be personal witnesses of his greatness and glory — in short, we become perfect by being devoted children. Trustful children don't shrink back wondering if they belong — which is actually an insult to the Father's grace. That is not the issue. The issue is, since God is my Father, how shall I honor his fatherhood?

Your relationship to God may be rooted in fear if:

1. You need to stay in control of what happens between you and God.
2. You struggle a lot with obedience.

3. Other sheep may hear his voice, but you don't.

4. You have little sincere desire to be close to God, for fear of what you might experience if you do.

One reason Christians rooted in fear have difficulty yielding to God is because they are unsure of God's motives. Suspicion always lurks in the background: "What do you really want from me?" "What will God let happen to me if I obey?" If we feel insecure with someone, we are always in self-protect mode with them. This in turn makes it difficult to know them as they really are.

Our best illustration of this truth is the Hebrews in the wilderness with Moses, who mistrusted God so much that they refused to enter the Promised Land. After encountering giant people and obstacles they didn't expect, they defaulted to believing God was motivated by something other than faithful love for them — perhaps he was just too interested in doing his God stuff to care if they got hurt in the process? Their view and judgment of God's character became totally perverted when viewed through the fear filter. They later accused God to Moses, that he had brought them out to the wilderness to let them die. Nothing was further from the truth, but in their need to assign a reason as to why their promised land didn't look like they thought it would, they chose to believe the worst about God's motives. I honestly have a little dread of what I will learn in heaven about the times I denied myself a great blessing from God because I didn't trust Him.

There is no fear in love

The heart rooted in love is free, because it is not cluttered with other motives. Loving someone more than ourselves liberates the heart from many a bondage. When a loving heart hears God's command, it doesn't stop to ponder: "What will this do to me?" Instead, the one rooted in love can say:

I run in the path of your commands, for you have set my heart free. (Psalm 119:32)

> **Your only hope of becoming a perfect son or daughter of God is to rest in God's love for you.**

Love does a work in the human soul that nothing else can. The one who lives in dreadful fear never comes to the completeness and perfection that love alone can work in him. The Apostle John was referring to this fact when he wrote in 1 John 4:18:

There is no fear in love — dread does not exist; but full-grown (complete, perfect) love turns fear out of doors and expels every trace of terror. For fear brings with it the thought of punishment, and so he who is afraid has not reached the full maturity of love — is not yet grown into love's complete perfection. (The Amplified Bible)

Your only hope of becoming a perfect (mature, full-grown) son or daughter of God is to throw off your fear and choose to rest in God's love for you. Anxious thoughts about what God thinks of you should be exchanged for believing what God says in his Word about his love for you. The issue of what God thinks of you should be settled in your heart. The greatest sin we can commit against God is not believing his Word including that one which says:

"How great is the love the Father has lavished on us, that we should be called children of God! And that is what we are!" 1 John 3:1

The Root of Ambition

Is your Christian life nagged by a pressure to perform? Do you fear losing God's love if you don't do it right? Is your religious life driven by trying to achieve success or prosperity? Is your prayer time used to know God better, or mostly for claiming your blessings? If any of these are true for you, you may be rooted in what the Bible calls selfish ambition.

Those rooted in selfish ambition have been taught to approach God and his Word as a formula for success, a means to reach their potential, or a heavenly path to prosperity. Christian bookshelves and conferences are filled with teaching on how to be a successful Christian, how to prosper, get your healing, how to get the anointing, and on and on. The casual observer might get the impression that Christianity's main purpose is to ensure your personal success.

For others, selfish ambition takes the form of a subtle turning aside from a calling to full-time ministry in service to God, towards the need to find one's identity and success in that ministry. There is a big difference, and in this chapter I will attempt to help you recognize that difference.

Love is perfection, but perfection is not love.

The selfishly ambitious Christian is still at the center of his own universe, instead of his God. He appears to be very spiritual at first glance, but is actually self-ish: self-centered, self-conscious, self-righteous. By the way Jesus responded to them, we know that many of the Pharisees, scribes and priests of his day were rooted in ambition.

This ambition may indeed be "spiritual" ambition — the desire to set an example for excellence in the Christian community, or achieve religious perfection. At first glance this goal appears to be noble, but can easily become a tool of the enemy who wants to pervert your hunger to be righteous and pleasing to God.

The devil knows he can't easily tempt committed Christians to steal, commit adultery, or any of those "big sins," so he takes another tack: he uses your God-given desire to be righteous against you by helping you turn it into a self-serving quest for perfection. This keeps the believer from knowing God, from entering into the sacred romance — which is where true life is found. In short, when you pursue perfection, the target shifts from God to yourself.

Authentic transformation and perfection is the fruit of a life shared with God, not the result of working oneself over. The genuine lover of God is not easily led astray, while the one who pursues perfection for perfection's sake will find himself off of that narrow path of life, on his way to somewhere else.

The soul who really loves God is not easily manipulated or deceived by the devil, because his personal success or failure is not an issue. The temptation of Jesus is our prime example: Satan tempted him with success as a religious leader and as a powerful ruler. God had destined Jesus for that very thing, which Jesus knew full well; but his goal was to love his Father faithfully, not make his own destiny happen. It was love for the Father that enabled Jesus to pass that temptation by and which set him on the path to real fulfillment of his destiny.

> **When you pursue perfection, the target shifts from God to yourself.**

The truth is that no one wants you to fulfill your created potential more than God. God has promised you abundant life and prosperity, and as his child these things become yours in a shared life of mutual faithfulness. He has a plan and a destiny for you. Yet if these things are the goal of your relationship rather than the joy of knowing God Himself, you risk developing a perverted relationship to God, where you become rooted in the desire to be successful rather than loving God.

Who are you being righteous for?

Though it may look identical outwardly, there is a tremendous difference between living righteously as a display of your love for God, and living righteously as a means to advance yourself. In the first case, your eyes are on the Lord, and you are relatively unconcerned about yourself. In the second case, performance and perfection become the focus of your Christian life — in other words, what you do, you do for your sake — your reputation, your status in the eyes of others, even your status in God's eyes. Paul complained about those who *"preach Christ out of selfish ambition, not sincerely..."* [Philippians 1:17].

The Christian rooted in spiritual ambition is loaded down with prayer formulas, success confessions and whatever current strategies an "overcomer" must follow. He is more likely to spend his extra money on books, teaching CD's or conferences than buy his lonely neighbor a nice meal — unless that act is part of the current formula for Christians-Who-Do-It-Right.

What motivates your choices?

We all want to be good Christians, but why do we want this? Are we seeking spiritual achievement as a means to feel successful as a human being? If so, it is a form of self-righteousness, an expression of the desire to glorify ourselves rather than glorify God — it is about us, and not about Him at all.

Jesus often pointed out that this was what motivated the Pharisees; that they did all the right religious things, but had no true love of God in their hearts. They didn't do their devotional acts because they loved the Father, but because they loved themselves. They loved to be successful, and therefore were full of spiritual ambition.

How do you know if you are rooted in spiritual ambition?

You may have become rooted in ambition or spiritual perfectionism if:

1. You've come to rely on faith confessions more than simple fellowship with the Lord to walk in strength.

2. When you are sick or weak or in need — especially prolonged — you don't want to confess it to anyone, because you fear being seen as a failure to your Christian peers.

3. Your giving is always with an eye on its reward (from man or God). No giving just for the joy of it.

4. You feel dissatisfied when not being used, or given a (possibly well-deserved) position. When you are being used, it bugs you to be unseen and unappreciated.

5. You feel jealous if another Christian is given more recognition or threatened by their spiritual gifts.

6. Prayer time is mostly for confessing your sins and lack of perfection to God.

7. You are very self-conscious and worry about how you appear to others, afraid to let them see your needs and weaknesses.

8. It is hard for you to relax and just enjoy being God's child.

The person rooted in spiritual ambition is driven to do spiritual works to earn love and favor. He has a hard time understanding why less hard-working Christians seem to be so blessed or happy. It is Martha being envious of Mary.

This person feels a continual need to prove himself and may be deeply concerned about what others think. They tend to follow successful people and may be easily deceived by those who teach wrong doctrines if they value success more than truth. The one rooted in love is not so easily deceived, because the love of God's truth is more important than the opinions of others.

The one rooted in selfish ambition may fail God suddenly, to the great surprise of himself and others. Think of Peter and the disciples, who swore their undying love, then failed Jesus in his greatest hour of need. They could neither stay awake and pray nor risk being identified with him as a political criminal; following him wasn't the path of success anymore. Their professions of love for Jesus were sincere enough, but they were powerless to pay the price that true love demands. Their actions reveal that their higher agenda or motivation was their own safety and/or success.

Navel gazing instead of beholding God

The Christian motivated by spiritual ambition is completely self-conscious, while giving the appearance of (even convincing himself that he is) being God conscious. He spends much time "navel gazing," self-inspecting for imperfection. Most of his time with God isn't spent enjoying God as much as continually confessing what is wrong with him. Such behavior on Israel's part caused God to cry out:

> *"You have not brought any fragrant calamus for me, or lavished on me the fat of your sacrifices. But you have burdened me with your sins and wearied me with your offenses." Isaiah 43:24*

"Sacrifices" here refers to God's ordained burnt offering, where one offered himself in devotion to God through a representative animal sacrifice; it was a worship offering, not a sin offering. When God complains that the believer has not "lavished on me the fat of your sacrifices," he is essentially saying: "You have not given yourself to me in fellowship and worship. You haven't come to celebrate the joy of our relationship or to strengthen it."

Likewise, the spiritually ambitious Christian may make a career out of confessing his sins and examining himself constantly, while never simply giving himself — his time and attention and devotion — to God.

Another example of spiritual ambition is the Christian who makes much ado about denying himself everything. While appearing to be totally humble, this Christian may actually take great pride in the perfection of emptying himself of all desire and denying himself any form of material blessing. To such a person any desire of the human heart is wrong, in himself and in others.

The Christian is undoubtedly called to take up his cross and deny himself to follow Christ — but the key here is "to follow Christ." Denying oneself everything just to earn a spiritual merit badge does not honor God, and it may dishonor the God who wants to pour out blessings on his child, who may have placed desires right in that child's heart (where he now lives) — and which he wants to guide that child to see fulfilled for the sake of his name and his glory, and their mutual joy.

Love's antidote to ambition and perfectionism

The heart motivated by love is dancing to a different tune. It is doing a passionate and abandoned tango, not a tortuous limbo that gets more difficult the longer the music plays. There is contentment, a sense of rest and peace about this Christian. This heart is satisfied in just being God's child, in experiencing his deep love and acceptance. He may also be a hard worker, but he doesn't do it to win the favor of God or man, he does it because he loves God and man. The issue of what God thinks of him is settled in his heart, because he is rooted in God's love for him, and everything is seen in the context of that powerful love.

The Christian rooted in love is not perfect, but neither is he anxious about his imperfection. He has been freed from self-consciousness because the question of his worth and value in God's sight has been settled by Christ and the Word of God, and he believes. Self-esteem is no longer the agenda behind his actions and he is less tempted with the need to impress others.

> The heart that is ambitious to love God well, will be kept safe from the ambition that serves self.

The heart rooted in love doesn't obey God in order to make brownie points in heaven, but because it delights him to please the one he loves. The heart rooted in love is much more likely to ask God what He wants and to do it promptly and fearlessly, than the ambitious Christian, because he knows that God is looking for the devoted heart, not for perfect performance. Believing this, he doesn't shrink back in fear that he won't do it right. He knows he is not serving a harsh taskmaster, but a Father whose heart is full of grace and compassion towards him. When this heart hears God's command, it doesn't have to stop and ponder the whys and wherefores of an anxious, performance-based mind.

Because of all the above, the life of this Christian is more likely to display a quiet but obvious power. The surrendered lover of God is more powerful because the Holy Spirit doesn't have to wrestle with him to do his will. In fact, God can even rest in the heart of such a one. Instead of the believer and the Lord always wrestling with one another, all the energies of the Holy Spirit in this person can be spent building his kingdom in and through this person, in his heart, in his home, and wherever he goes. The heart that is ambitious to love God well, will be kept safe from the ambition that serves self.

The Root of Law

Does Christianity feel much more like a list of do's and don'ts to be followed, than an interactive relationship with a real (though invisible) Person? Are you more comfortable following the Ten Commandments than following Holy Spirit? Do you feel like it is a sin to do anything outside of church or denominational tradition? You may be rooted in law, or legalism.

The Pharisees of Jesus day were mostly rooted in religious tradition, or strict adherence to their interpretation of the laws of God. The law was not the problem; the law was given by God, and the Hebrews from Old Testament times had been instructed through Moses, Joshua and others to follow it carefully. However, down through the centuries the priesthood (the forerunners to the Pharisees) added to the law what became their own traditions, traditions that gradually wandered far from the heart of God who gave the original law.

Eventually, the Pharisees were so entirely focused on the law and on their traditions, that they did not recognize God in Jesus — who was the Word made flesh — the very one they were looking for, as the Messiah. Jesus fulfilled and embodied all of their original Torah, but they could not see this because they were so focused on the Torah, the law, itself. This would be like clinging to a map of Hawaii instead of getting out and experiencing Hawaii itself.

Loving the law more than the lawgiver.

Those who have zeal for the Word of God while not focused on honoring the Living Person of God may come to interpret the Word in a way that is not a faithful representation of the heart of God. This is what we call legalism, or a love for the law that ignores the values and purposes of the One who made it so that in fact, the lawgiver Himself is dishonored.

Those rooted in tradition often believe that encounters with God outside of their doctrinal traditions are illegitimate. For them God is unknowable and unrecognizable apart from their familiar structures; their faith is actually in rules and doctrines more than in God Himself. One can become focused so much on the outward sacraments and forms in the church that one misses the grace of God and the realities of relationship illustrated and celebrated by those sacraments.

Two people can participate in the same religious ritual with very different motives. One is a worshiper, the other a performer. One will be deeply aware of God's purpose in it and be drawn into worship of God, while the other may not actually worship God at all. The latter may even be quite confident that he has pleased God in practicing the ritual, without actually giving his heart to God at all. The latter Christian is self-centered, the former is God centered. Often only God knows the difference.

Rituals are not an end in themselves; their purpose is to bring us face-to-face with God Himself, acting as a sort of spiritual bungee cord to bring our wandering hearts back to God; or to bring us into a season of grateful remembrance for what God has done. Religious traditions are predictable and safe. Relationships can be unpredictable, especially when trying to relate to an invisible God. Rules, on the other hand, are much less personal. It feels

> **Two people can participate in the same religious ritual with very different motives. One is a worshiper, the other a performer.**

very different to break a rule than it does to disappoint or refuse a person.

Like the one rooted in ambition, the legalist feels pressure to be perfect, to perform. The main difference between a legalist and an ambitious Christian is that the legalist may actually be more concerned with pleasing God, while the ambitious person just wants to make a success of his life, and has found a formula (Christianity) to do so.

The Pharisees were rooted in tradition and the observance of the law because they enjoyed the "righteousness" produced by their own works. They were quite sure that their perfect observance of the law would please God more than being gracious to one who had fallen into sin. They had long since lost sight of the fact that the original Ten Commandments instructed them in what righteousness looks like between man and God, and between man and man. God has always been focused on relationship, which is the only arena that matters for the display of glory and righteousness. God's glory is most clearly revealed in relationship. Jesus understood this and was underscoring this truth when he said,

> *"Woe to you, teachers of the law and Pharisees, you hypocrites! You give a tenth of your spices — mint, dill and cumin. But you have neglected the more important matters of the law — justice, mercy and faithfulness. You should have practiced the latter, without neglecting the former." Matthew 23:23*

The Pharisees were so focused on observing the law that they not only failed to understand God's heart, they continually offended and grieved the Lord they claimed so confidently to please; their teaching about God became perverted, inaccurate, and ultimately an unfaithful witness to who God really is. This is why they taught their disciples that it was all right to be unkind to their parents in order to obey their traditions; why they were sure God would rather they observe the Sabbath rest with utter strictness than exert oneself in helping the sick or needy. Thus Jesus was always at odds with them, because he wanted to show people the truth about his Father's heart. Jesus healed people on the Sabbath because it was the right thing to do. But the Pharisees were infuriated, a reaction which revealed that they neither loved God nor the people whom God loved.

The law points to our goal; it is not the goal.

The Word of God reveals the will of God. It is truly flawless, and should be obeyed. In his time on earth, Jesus perfectly modeled for us the heart that is motivated by love and fulfills the law in doing so. When Jesus refused to stone the woman caught in the act of adultery, he was the only one standing there who was actually qualified to cast the first stone, but he did not, even though the law given by his own Father (to Moses) required it. How did he know the righteous thing to do in that moment in order to fulfill the law? He told us in the gospel of John, *"I only do and say what my Father tells me to do and say."* He revealed that he wasn't following rules, he was following a Person. As a human being on earth, he did that through the same means we have been given: with the help of the Holy Spirit.

Think about this: the Ark had the Ten Commandments inside, the laws that revealed God's values and how to live faithfully in a covenant with God and man; but the Law was covered by the mercy seat, and God lived above the mercy seat. This pictures for us that God's people are not meant to be face-to-face with the laws, but with the presence of God Himself. If the Hebrews had taken those engraved tablets out of the ark to worship them, ignoring God's presence in favor of focusing on the Ten Commandments, they would have likewise dishonored God. This is legalism: exalting law above the Lawgiver.

The law is good, and we need it; but we need it as a teacher, not as a basis for relationship. Only sincere love for God and others will instruct us in the wise and good way to apply the law. Indeed, as love becomes stronger, it makes the law unnecessary.

> **If you are in Christ, your job is not to follow rules, it is to follow a Person.**

On any given Sunday there are likely to be more sermons on how to follow the "rules" of Christianity than on how to love the Lord, more focus on religious tradition than honoring and yielding to the Holy Spirit, who is God with us [2 Corinthians 3:17]. Please know — and remind your Christian brothers and sisters — that if you are in Christ, your job is not to follow rules, it is to follow a Person.

You may be rooted in the law or religious tradition if:

1. You have been discipled with a focus on the rules of Christianity or the doctrines of your particular denomination.

2. You're pretty sure God is only pleased with you if you follow those rules, and when you don't do it just right, you feel guilty — which is most of the time.

3. It is hard for you not to judge others who, in your opinion, aren't following the rules.

4. You believe it is wrong to focus on the Holy Spirit's presence and guidance since we have the Scriptures to live by. You are much more comfortable sticking with what the Bible says about God than trying to know an invisible God living right within you.

5. You find it very hard to approach God in prayer unless you have done everything just right.

The truth is that the law is good, and we need it. But we need it only as a teacher, not as a basis for relationship. The law teaches us how love should behave, until we know how to love. The simple perversion we so easily slip into is that we make the law our focus, rather than the motive to love. When our motive is to love, we naturally and easily do what the law requires. But when our goal is to be perfect at doing the law, love for others (including God) is trumped by performance. The focus of your heart will be "How does my religious report card look?" rather than "How can I love you?"

Those rooted in law have difficulty understanding the grace of God because they still believe righteousness is something they can and must achieve for themselves. They have not realized how truly bankrupt and helpless they are without the help of the Holy Spirit, nor have they truly accepted the fact that in God's eyes, they stand with Jesus in his sight, sharing in his favor and righteousness.

> Those rooted in law ask, "How does my religious report card look?" rather than "How can I love you?"

This is the free gift that a legalist never unwraps and keeps trying to buy, but never has enough money. The one who has never been established in God's love never feels comfortable with drawing near to the Lord in intimacy, because his heart says that privilege is only for those who perfectly follow the rules, and he's pretty sure he is not that person.

The Blessing of Benjamin

The reason we become rooted in law is because we hunger for self-righteousness. God wants us to hunger for HIM, to experience and partake of and trust in HIS righteousness. You do this by coming to Him as a helpless and trusting child comes to a good and wise Father, learning from his love, how to love.

Our relationship to God is described beautifully in Deuteronomy 33:12, which is the blessing Moses bestowed upon the tribe of Benjamin:

> *"Let the beloved of the Lord rest secure in him, for he shields him all day long, and the one the Lord loves rests between his shoulders."*

This is what I call the snuggle blessing. As the youngest of the twelve sons of Jacob, the proverbial "baby of the family," Benjamin always represents for us the one who is childlike with God, who is the favored one, the Little One towards whom the father feels particularly tender and protective. Moses' words may also remind you of the moment when John leaned against Jesus at their shared meal. It is the picture of intimate familiarity, of relaxing into and resting against the Lord without any rules, laws or traditions standing between them. It portrays comfortable, confident, presumptuous love.

Interestingly enough, the Apostle Paul was of the tribe of Benjamin, and one who prided himself on being "a Pharisee among Pharisees." But after his encounter with Christ on the Damascus Road, it became clear from his letters that Paul had finally entered into the blessing of Benjamin: he rested in God's love, he came to know God as adoring Father instead of Cosmic Judge, who would go on to exhort us all to "Be imitators of God, therefore, *as dearly loved children.*" [Ephesians 5:1] He also wrote to the church at Rome: *Love is the fulfillment of the law. [13:10].* Paul successfully made the transition from rules to relationship, from law to love. Sincere love for God leads the child of God to naturally abandon the work of religion and rest in the arms of God.

Only love can overthrow legalism in a Christian. We must be first rooted and established in the love of God before we can successfully go another step in life with Him.

My Introduction To The Love of God

In my years as a pastor's wife I've come to believe that a change of heart or a changed mind is the greatest miracle God works. It is easier for most of us to believe God will heal the blind than to believe he can change someone's mind. Paul was dramatically impacted by the blinding light on the road and his encounter with the Lord, but his character was not transformed completely in that instant. Transformation is a process, and love is God's favorite means.

In spite of being born into a family of Southern Baptists, I managed to grow up knowing very little about Jesus. My parents divorced when I was six, and I was primarily raised by my mother. After her own Southern Baptist upbringing, my mother, who was hungry for abundant life, became disillusioned with "organized religion" like so many of her generation, put off by the hypocrisy she often saw in Christians. She did not stop believing in God, but having never known God in any context apart from church tradition, she was left hungry for the real love and goodness the Scriptures promised of God and prescribed for his people. Not finding it in church, and weary of the rules, her soul wandered off to find life elsewhere.

As I grew up, I absorbed Mom's attitude about religious people, assuming that they were at worst hypocritical rule followers, at best constricted away from all that made life lively. No fun, too many rules, I assumed. Mother loved life; I love life. I wanted it to the full — doesn't everyone? In the early sixties, when the quest for personal freedom was erupting everywhere — between the races, in the home, between the sexes

— church didn't seem the place to find real life. I thought religion would only ruin my fun, so I held it and God Himself at arm's length.

Many summers I visited my Baptist cousin, a fun-loving girl my age. But the price for that fun was always the same: trekking back and forth to the church all week. Annually on a summer Sunday morning her Baptist preacher declared me to be a sinner, while my heart protested, "I am not! I'm a good person!" After lunch and a too-short afternoon, we always went back to church Sunday night to attend Training Union, then back again on Wednesday night. By the end of our visits I was relieved that I didn't have to go to church all the time like my cousin did, happy that I was free. I treasured my freedom, as my mother had treasured hers — so much that she divorced my father in 1956 in order to explore that freedom fully in search of the life she wanted.

The summer of my 12th year, my grandmother Blanche broke through my resistance to God, ever so briefly. After she witnessed to me about Jesus, knelt with her by the bed and asked Him to save me. It was a very heartfelt experience, full of conviction and tears. However, after we returned home and I went back to the preoccupations of my pre-teen life, that moment faded so thoroughly I forgot it ever happened. One time out of curiosity I pulled my mother's dusty King James Bible off the shelf, but couldn't understand any of it and just put it back. (Looking back now, that act was a perfect snapshot of my salvation experience as well.) So I grew up without any remembrance of the event; I didn't feel saved and certainly didn't act like it for the next 17 years.

As I approached adulthood and the promise of independence, I dreamed of having a great life and becoming a happy, productive person. I wanted to have what every woman wants: a life with beauty, romance, family, purpose and fun. I spent my 20's going after that, until one day when I was 29 I realized my life had none of that, in spite of all my efforts. One summer morning I was overwhelmed with the realization of how empty and ugly my heart and life had become, so much that I ended up on the floor in a fetal crouch, weeping uncontrollably, and all alone. All the freedom I had guarded so carefully had been used to make choices that had actually robbed me of the life I had once dreamed of, and for the first time I was seeing the connection. I was my own worst enemy, and I hated myself for it. I was awash in hopelessness, grief and shame.

My latest exercise of freedom in search of the great life had been to divorce my husband. All my life I had blamed everyone else for my unhappiness, beginning with my mother. It was always someone else's fault that I wasn't having an abundant life. My ex-husband was the most recent target of my blame, but on this day, months after breaking free of him, life was still deeply unsatisfying and there was no one else to blame.

> All the freedom I had guarded so carefully had been used to make choices that had actually robbed me of the life I had once dreamed of.

Now I was a single mother trying to raise two children by myself, and I had ripped my family apart. I had never felt so utterly alone in my life, and now I had a horrible new clarity that I was the one who had created that life. I was seeing myself really for the first time, and was sick at heart over who I had become: a selfish, foolish woman with morals and values that changed with the winds of my need.

As I cried my heart out that day, I desperately longed for someone to come and take care of me, to make it all right, to make me all right. My children were visiting their father for a week, so I was totally alone for the first time in my life. Trying to escape my feelings, I tried repeatedly to call my best friend, but got no answer. I called another friend whose line was busy for hours; and two other friends didn't answer the phone, either. This cycle of weeping and phone dialing went on all that Saturday morning.

Even my new Christian friend didn't answer. At a new job begun a few months earlier, I had been befriended by Margaret, one of those cheerful Christians who loved to take any opportunity in a conversation to say, "Jesus loves you!" One day, seeing that I was struggling after my divorce, she gave me her pastor's card in case I needed some counseling. I threw it in my purse with zero intention of ever calling him. I tolerated her talk of God and church, but as always, kept my guard up against being drug into the religious scene.

But I was so sick at heart that awful morning that I allowed myself to consider God in earnest, for the first time. Was he real? Did he really love me in a personal way like Margaret said, even though I was, I now realized, not a good person at all? Still, I was determined to not talk myself into believing what she said. I refused to make myself believe in a God I couldn't see or a love I couldn't feel.

Finally I felt so desperate that I challenged God, in case he was real and just might be paying attention. Lying on the floor, through tears I shook my fist towards heaven and said, "God, if you're really real, if you're really all powerful, then you're going to have to make me feel this love I keep hearing about. I'm not going to talk myself into it!"

Nothing happened. No thunderbolts, no music, no feelings. I finally cried myself out and got up from the floor. As I walked past my purse in the kitchen I remembered the pastor's card for the first time in weeks. I found it buried under crumpled receipts and cigarette crumbles in the bottom of my purse and dialed the number, though I didn't really expect a preacher to answer the phone on a Saturday. After all, they only work on Sundays and Wednesdays, right?

But the pastor did answer the phone, and offered to meet me in a couple of hours. I really didn't want to go, but felt like I had to talk to someone; I couldn't bear to be alone with myself. I really hoped he wasn't one of those holier-than-thou types, and was greatly relieved when he emerged from his office wearing jeans and a paint-stained sweatshirt.

Not caring what he thought of me, I began to pour my heart out to him, revealing every awful thing I could think of about myself, and how I had come to hate the woman who was sitting there before him. He didn't seem put off or shocked by any of my confessions. He didn't try to lead me to Jesus or preach to me; he didn't even counsel me much, just listened intently and assured me that God did love me and would forgive me if I asked. He prayed for me and gave me a paperback Good News Bible. I went home a bit comforted and emotionally exhausted. I had not told the pastor about my challenge to God, but I felt better for having unloaded my conscience; after all, if I was going to even think about letting God into my life, it was only fair that He know everything about me right up front.

The next morning I agreed to attend church with Margaret, but I made her sit on the back row so I could escape without too much embarrassment if I got uncomfortable. To be honest, I didn't go with any real hope in experiencing God; it was mostly curiosity and that lingering dread of being alone with myself another day.

The service was pleasant enough, and I have no idea what the preacher preached, but as we stood to our feet to sing the closing hymn, something happened that had nothing to do with songs or sermons: the most intense feeling of being loved washed over me. It was the most powerful feeling I had ever known. One couldn't make this kind of thing up, and I certainly wasn't trying. If anything, I was on the cautious defensive with God, but this wave of love leaped over every defense I had. In fact, that love felt just like an ocean wave, a sensation I knew very well.

God couldn't have found a more personal way to let me experience his love, because having grown up on the Texas coast I had laid at the surf's edge many times and let the breakers wash up over me. I had always admired the majestic power of the waves and marveled at the combination of strength and gentleness I felt as they flowed over my body at the shoreline. You can't stop an ocean wave; it is too powerful. That morning, God's love washed over me just like that, and I could no more ignore his love than I could have stopped one of those ocean waves.

I was so stunned and amazed by the sensation that I didn't know how to act. Knowing the service was almost over, I ran out the back door of the church, not wanting to be in the midst of strangers while I was feeling such intense and unfamiliar emotions. Tears were pouring out of me again, but now not from despair. They were the irrepressible overflow of an unfamiliar joy I felt in the presence of this Jesus I did not know.

As I hurried down the sidewalk I heard the door open behind me and a voice saying, "Oh no you don't, you're not getting away from me this time!" I stopped on the sidewalk, and the arms of my friend Margaret encircled me from behind, but I knew with all my formerly unbelieving heart that those were the words and arms of Jesus, that he wanted me and loved me — sinful, hopeless, selfish me.

I did not have words for it then, but I do now: I was born anew in the love of God that day; an invisible event more real than any experience I'd ever had before. That moment is as vivid to me now as it was in August of 1979. God had answered my challenge: he had demonstrated both his power and his love, and I believed.

Galatians Chapter 3

What I didn't know then was that the kingdom of darkness goes on high alert when someone experiences God's love, because they know better than many humans that love is the means through which God builds his kingdom. As soon as the enemy of my soul noticed I was experiencing God's love, he did everything he could to thwart it. You see, just three or four hours after I experienced the ocean wave of God's love that so overwhelmingly convinced me of his presence, I was filled with doubt all over again. Had I really felt God's love? Was he really real? Home alone again that afternoon, lying on my bed, I thought perhaps I had imagined it all.

I picked up the paperback Bible the preacher had given me. I had never read a single page in the Bible, and had no idea where to begin. So I addressed God with another test that went something like this:

"God, if you're really there, then speak to me through whatever page I open and read in this Bible. Say something personal to me!" I wanted something to take me right back to that awesome love I had felt. I popped the book open and my eyes fell upon Galatians Chapter 3. I read hungrily, hoping for some personal message that would touch my heart again. But I didn't find it, and the words meant nothing to me. I was so disappointed. I tossed the Bible aside and cried myself to sleep.

> As soon as the enemy of my soul noticed I was experiencing God's love, he did everything he could to thwart it.

I awoke later to the phone ringing; my friend Margaret invited me to her Sunday night Bible study. Honestly, that was the last place I wanted to go; I knew I would be embarrassed in front of all those Christians who were familiar with their Bibles. Besides, I wasn't ready to plunge into this religious stuff. I feared that if I went back to that building with her again I would be sucked into the whole religious scene, trapped into obligatory meetings, prayer circles, Bible studies. All of the emptiness I felt towards God had returned, so all of me wanted to say no.

But I said yes, and I knew it was because I was so very lonely and desperate. Weekdays were safe because I could hide in my job as a legal secretary, which I enjoyed very much. Saturdays and Sundays, however, were the loneliest time in the world. I dreaded being alone worse than I feared being hooked by those Christians.

The class was informal: everyone had coffee or sodas and sat around the table in jeans and t-shirts. This surprised and relaxed me a bit, though I still wanted to be the invisible woman. The pastor walked in, greeted everyone and opened the class by saying, "Okay everybody, I hope you read your assignment for this week, Galatians Chapter 3." My heart exploded in joy! Forgetting myself, I jumped up, and gushed, "God got me ready for this! He IS real! This chapter is the only one in the Bible I've ever read, and I read it today!" I was amazed yet again, and everyone rejoiced with me.

God had been showing his love and power to me that afternoon, responding immediately to my test, but I couldn't see it because I was looking for something else. If I had not gone to that study, I would have missed the proof of God's personal love and responsiveness to my prayer. Instead of taking my loneliness away, he had used it to bring me to where I could see how he had been loving me in the midst of it.

It has been like that ever since. I fell in love with the Lord that night and gave my heart to this invisible Jesus. This holy and powerful God had stooped down to my level and had graciously submitted to my test, because he wanted me so much. I weep even as I write these words, remembering the joy of that first realization that the God of the universe loved me, was personally attentive to my needs and willing to meet me where I was.

> God had been showing his love and power to me, but I couldn't see it because I was looking for something else.

The enemy of my soul still tries to continually bring doubts about God's love, but whenever he does I step forward towards God in faith now. He always meets me and rewards my faith in his love. I began to sink my roots down into God's love that day, and began the process of being established in it as the source of my heart's nurture.

When I was at my worst moment as a human being, God came for me, and won me with his love. It was a love so real, so un-made-up on my part, so consistent, that I began to change out of joy and gratitude for this Person who pursued me, who valued me, who accepted me. Like most new believers, the initial changes I made in my way of life were simply a response to God's love. I was so grateful to Him that I naturally wanted to change my behavior, because his kind of love demands a response.

I was so flush with the first love I felt from God that no one had to make me go to church or read my Bible, I wanted to do these things. As one who had never been indoctrinated in religion, I read my Bible with fresh eyes of childlike wonder. I bought the whole package, so much so that I eventually married that preacher.

I am not a perfect Christian, but I am a deeply satisfied one. I enjoy his love for me, and today I enjoy loving Him in return. But it wasn't always so.

One-Sided Love Isn't His Plan

In the course of my first three years of being a Christian, the happiness of being loved by God gradually faded. One day it dawned on me that while I'd been immersing myself in being a pastor's wife, I had drifted into being one of those people I had avoided for so long: a joyless religious person who had very little real satisfaction in knowing God. I had never stopped appreciating what God had done for me, so there was always thankfulness in my heart, but I increasingly had to force myself in matters of prayer and study and church attendance. That is a serious problem for a pastor's wife.

When I read my Bible in those days, scriptures like this one really bugged me:

> *Love the Lord your God with all your heart and with all your soul and with all your mind and with all your strength. (Mark 12:30).*

I knew I didn't love Jesus like this; yet Scripture often spoke of drawing near to God with a heart full of passion for Him, and it seemed every time I opened the Bible I encountered one of these. I tried to make myself feel this love for God by increasing prayer and Bible study, but these didn't change my feelings for God; they just made me more deeply aware of how dull my religious life now felt.

I knew life with God was based on faith, but it didn't sound to me like the Bible wanted me to just love God by faith; it seemed to me it taught that once I'd found faith IN

God I should then progress to something like real heartfelt love FOR Him. Not only did I not love God like this, I didn't know how to make myself do it. I wondered how anyone really did that.

I realized I needed more than a Bible, a church and good intentions to carry out the command to love Him. It seemed I had two choices: to settle for the dry toast dutiful Christian life — and the secret shame of not loving the Lord as I should — or figure out what piece of the puzzle was missing and beg for help. I decided to beg for help.

My plea went something like: "Lord, I really don't love you like this. To be honest, it's not even that high on my priority list. Jesus, I know it is right to love you like this, and I want to, but I don't know how. Please create in me the desire to love you, and show me how to keep this command."

Amazingly, I felt great relief after I confessed this to God. The fresh breeze of honesty between myself and God actually caused me to feel closer to Him immediately, and to my surprise, the sense of anxiety and shame I had been feeling was replaced with peace and hope. Not only did I now feel no condemnation, I actually sensed his deep approval and pleasure that I was concerned about being able to love Him.

(I understood much later that confession is a joy to God because from his standpoint, confession removes barriers of sin and guilt, opening the way for Him to fully embrace his child again, so that child can receive his strengthening help. Seeing our true state and confessing it draws out the compassionate Father who wants to help us. When we allow our sins and failures to cause us to hide from Him — as Adam did in Eden — then even if God wants to embrace us, we won't show up for it as long as we're hiding out somewhere.)

> Confessing our sins draws out the compassionate Father who wants to help us.

Searching for a way to sincerely love the Lord

As I pondered these things, the thought kept surfacing that in the Bible, it seemed God was always promising to provide the strength or ability needed to obey Him in anything. For instance, when he sent men to war, he would often promise to fight the battle for them. It wasn't unusual for Him to send his people to fight a much stronger adversary, and when they stepped out to obey, he would do something like put the enemy to sleep, or confuse them, so that his less powerful army won great victories. And I then "just happened" to read 2 Peter 1:3:

> *"His divine power has given us everything we need for life and godliness through our knowledge of him who called us by his own glory and goodness."*

I began to see that in order to obey the command to love God I needed a power I didn't have. While believing that God was the powerful creator of the universe, I still had no understanding of what it meant to experience God's power on a really personal level. I asked the Lord to show me how to connect with his power in the real ways needed to carry out what this love command required.

Within a few days, God arranged for me to learn of my need to be filled with the Holy Spirit, through some mature Christians and a book (that just appeared on our coffee table, I kid you not — and still don't know where it came from) called "Nine O'Clock In the Morning" by Episcopal priest Dennis Bennett.

I didn't know much about the Holy Spirit, but I was ready to trust what these other Christians and Rev. Bennett had to say because I saw that Jesus confirmed what they said in his teaching about the Holy Spirit, especially in the gospel of John. The Bible clearly taught that Jesus' followers needed to be baptized by Him with the Holy Spirit. How had I missed it before? Up until now, all my "god" focus had been on God the Father and God the Son; I had paid little attention to the Holy Spirit. I just knew this was God's answer to my cry for help. So I asked Jesus to baptize me in his Spirit, and he did.

Just as I had felt the overwhelming wave of God's love for me on that day, this time I now experienced an intense new love for the Lord! It was mysterious to me, but wonderful, and very real. You can't make this stuff up — believe me, I had really tried.

The Holy Spirit changed everything

After Jesus filled me with the Holy Spirit, everything changed. I was hungrier to know the Lord, and I really longed for Him, so I went to prayer more often, and with real expectation of encountering the Living God. Instead of just going down my list of prayer requests, I often enjoyed just sitting and resting in his presence. He seemed so near, and I sensed Him speaking in my spirit with a frequency, familiarity and ease I'd never known before. I felt, for the first time, like John leaning against the bosom of the Lord.

It also became easier to simply turn my attention upon Him and become aware of his presence as I went through the hours and activities of my day. When you truly adore someone, you want to be with them, share everything, know their thoughts and feelings, experience life with them. Love stirs in you a natural longing to do things for them, to serve them, to bless them. I just wanted to share life with God, and to discover more about Him, to get to know Him. For the first time since becoming a Christian I felt that God was truly sharing life with me. Of course, He had been with me all the time, but my ability to be aware of and respond to God had been inconsistent and feeble without the Holy Spirit.

I discovered that the Holy Spirit passionately loves the Father and the Son, and loves to help us do the same. Just as Jesus promised, the Holy Spirit is indeed the Helper who comes alongside us in this world. (This is taught in detail in the book

> The Holy Spirit passionately loves the Father and the Son, and loves to help us do the same.

entitled "Spirit Life" in this series.)

With his help, I learned to direct my affection towards the Lord and develop the intimacy I had read so much about. No matter what problems I faced on a given day, anxiety rarely stayed with me, as I tapped into the reliable peace and presence of the Holy Spirit. With that experience over 25 years behind me now, I know without a doubt that being filled with the Holy Spirit is the key to the promised treasure that is satisfying life with God. When your whole being is filled with the Holy Spirit, you begin to share life with God on a whole new level. I now believe this is meant to be the normal experience of every child of God.

I certainly didn't deserve to have God's love poured out on me that first day, but I do know why it happened: I cried out for it. And now I know that it was the Holy Spirit who came with that wave of love. Unquestionably, experiencing God's love (or wisdom or grace or strength) is impossible apart from the help of the Holy Spirit. Romans 5:5 teaches that the Holy Spirit is the one who brings the experience of God's love to you. I believe a primary reason why so many in the Body of Christ are not rooted in love is that they have not been fully taught about the vital role the Holy Spirit plays in their experience of God.

The power to love comes only from the Holy Spirit

We must rely upon the Holy Spirit in every part of the transaction of covenant love between us and God. It is his task to make known to you the limitless and powerful love of God, and to enable you to love God in return, so that you can share life with God in true covenant faithfulness. He loves God the

Father and Jesus the Son with a passionate pure love, and he love you the same way.

Remember that anything God commands — and in which you find yourself completely powerless — if you humbly confess your weakness to Him along with your desire to obey, his power will come to help you. That's just who this God is with whom we have been invited to share life. It's a partnership: your choice, his power. He won't choose for you, and you don't have the power to carry out your desire to obey, but when you choose his will, he provides the thing you cannot, the ability to carry it through. That's what Peter taught us in 2 Peter 1:3.

Like many others, perhaps you thought loving God was just hard because he is invisible and you can only know Him "by faith" — that it would be easier if only you could see Him. I invite you to consider those who first walked with the Lord, such as Peter, who brashly swore he loved Jesus enough to die for Him, yet denied he even knew Him three times as he went to the cross a short time later. He utterly failed to love Jesus in the hour of his greatest need, in spite of the fact that he knew Jesus face-to-face.

Though Jesus forgave his disciples, things did not change for them until after Jesus returned to heaven so they could receive the Father's promised gift — the Holy Spirit. After that encounter we see Peter and the disciples going about in a new power. They not only performed great miracles, but history tells us that most of them endured persecution with strength and joy, displaying a powerful love for Jesus that never failed over the course of many years. What was the difference? It was the Holy Spirit: He is the one who enabled them to love God with an unfailing love, to take them beyond their desires and good intentions. The Holy Spirit is the one Paul refers to in Ephesians 3:20 as he speaks of *"him who is able to do immeasurably more than all we ask or imagine, according to his power that is at work within us..."*

First Steps To Being Established In Love

"...Being rooted and established in love..." Such a small phrase, but one of the most important ones in the Bible. So many Christians wrestle with experiencing the powerful love of God. How does one become rooted in love? How does one come to know how much God loves him, and experience this love in all its fullness, and then develop the ability to love God in return? It won't happen the same for everyone, but I can tell you how it happened for me. But first, I want to give you a little framework in which to organize all the things I will be sharing in the pages to come.

Covenant, Childlikeness and Rest

In the years since I was first captivated by God's love, the three most important things I have learned about being a Christian are that:

(1) Through the blood of Christ we are invited to share life with God in a covenant of mutual unfailing love;

(2) My role in this covenant is to live by faith in being a beloved child of God and living worthy of that honor;

(3) God calls this life "entering rest," something we can only do by receiving, trusting and relating to his covenant gift, the Holy Spirit.

Our life in Christ is called the new covenant of Jesus. The benefits of this covenant are first described in Jeremiah 31:31–34, where God declares his promise to redeem his people from their slavery. The same promises are quoted in Hebrews 8:10-12 to verify that these are indeed the blessings of the covenant offered to us through Jesus Christ. So Christianity is not merely a religion or membership in church; it is a covenant of unfailing love. Covenant love is a forever commitment that is not based on a feeling, but upon the choice and faithfulness of the lover.

This covenant promises to those who put faith in Jesus Christ that they:

- Will be forgiven of sin;

- Will be able to know God, regardless of status, race, gender, or education;

- Will be personally taught by God.

Sadly, most people have been taught to focus on "the rules" of Christianity instead of being educated about the covenant promises God makes to those who become his family. The most amazing thing to me is the promise that we will all know God, which implies that he wants to be known by us, not just rule over us from on high. "Knowing" includes everything involved in relating to anyone: hearing his voice, experiencing his personality, his wisdom, being privy to his thoughts. In case you have any doubts about God's intention, consider that Paul wrote of these very things in 1 Corinthians 2:9-16 and explained that these thing are why we have been given the Holy Spirit, for He is the one who, as the Spirit of Christ, enables us to know Christ in ways not possible for a mere human being.

> **Christianity is not merely a religion or membership in church; it is a covenant of unfailing love.**

Having laid that foundation, I will share my experience of being established in God's love.

First, learn God's love language.

My pastor counseled me to begin my study of God's word in the four New Testament Gospels, plus the Psalms and Proverbs. I read in these daily. This is the most excellent advice to a new believer — or any believer who wants to know God better — because one learns about the character, motives and power of Jesus in the gospels; the Psalms read like the journals of real men in all of their joy, worship, disappoint or struggles in relating to God; and one learns practical wisdom for every matter of daily life from the Proverbs.

The Psalms in particular are laced with the language of God's love; I read them daily, still after 30 years. And in case I've convinced you to make this your habit, I want to teach you about one very important word in connection with God's love, *chesed*, the Hebrew word for committed covenant love. Because of this it is one of the most important words in the Old Testament. It is used 241 times, mostly in the Psalms; an example is found in Psalm 32:10:

> *Many are the woes of the wicked, but the Lord's unfailing love surrounds the man who trusts in him.*

The phrase "unfailing love" here has been translated from *chesed*. This is the normal phrase used in the New International Version to express *chesed*. The reason I take time to show you this is that in most original translations (such as King James, New American Standard, and Revised Standard) *chesed* is usually translated as mercy, lovingkindness, or covenant kindness. Even though these words are an accurate translation of the Hebrew meaning for *chesed*, the problem is that the words "kindness" and "mercy" don't carry the same meaning in our culture as they did in the days of Abraham, Moses and David. Frankly, words like "kindness" and "mercy" have little impact when we hear them.

First, our culture is very different than that of the ancient Hebrews; second, within any culture, the meanings attached to words change over time. It is easy to think of several words we use in America today whose meaning is very different than it was 10, 20 or 30 years ago. What I like about the NIV is that the translators recognized this fact and translated the original Hebrew as it most closely conveys THEIR meaning for US today, which is a commitment to love another without fail, forever. They called it covenant kindness, but if we use the word kindness we'd never get the impact of this amazing word. In our culture "kindness" or "mercy" do little to capture the real meaning of the word.

A few other examples of *chesed* are:

> *The Lord loves righteousness and justice; the earth is full of his unfailing love. (Psalm 33:5).*

> *But the eyes of the Lord are on those who fear him, on those whose hope is in his unfailing love... (Psalm 33:18).*

> *May your unfailing love rest upon us, O Lord, even as we put our hope in you. (Psalm 33:22).*

Moses used *chesed* in Psalm 90:14 when he asked God to *"satisfy us in the morning with your unfailing love..."* — one of my favorite prayers. This is the love we are meant to rest in as we share life with God.

We also find this word represented in the New Testament, when Jesus quotes from Hosea 6:6:

> *"But go and learn what this means: 'I desire mercy, not sacrifice.' For I have not come to call the righteous, but sinners." Matthew 9:13*

In Hosea 6:6 the word "mercy" is *chesed*. Jesus quoted Hosea to point out yet again that faithful committed love is more important than all religious activity.

Whatever Bible translation you use, never forget that Old Testament words like kindness and mercy nearly always refer to the unfailing love that God promises those who put faith in Christ and the "blood of the new covenant" [1 Corinthians 11:25].

We went through that little word exercise because I told you my first step in being established in God's love was to learn God's love language.

Second, study and Believe God's Word

My pastor husband, having observed my growth in the things of God from the very beginning, says I grew faster than anyone he had ever seen. I don't believe this rapid growth came because I was special or stronger than anyone else. I believe it happened because I chose to believe from the beginning that God divinely inspired the Scriptures, instead of allowing myself to become a judge of what to believe and what not to believe. Thus I got the full impact of his Word; it was never watered down for me. I accepted what God said with all the authority he intended it to carry as truth that would govern my life and behavior.

I also believe I grew quickly because very simply, I believed what God said about his love for me, and lived like I believed it. Like the parable of the mustard seed, my feeble faith, once buried in the rich soil of God's love, grew into a mighty tree. To simply read the Bible and take it at face value as the expression of God's heart resulted in many wonderful things. The issue of his love was settled in my heart — not only did I believe it to be true, but that his love is meant to

> The Bible said I could hear my Lord's voice; I did. It said He would satisfy the hunger of my heart; He has.

be something experienced up close and personal. Because of what the Bible said, I believed God was aware of my every thought and need, and that his love and attention was ready to be personally expressed in my daily life.

The Bible said I could hear my Lord's voice; I did. It said He would satisfy the hunger of my heart; He has, as often as I offered that hunger to Him. The Bible said I needed the Father's gift, the Holy Spirit, in order to live the life he offered. When I understood that fact, I received his gift without fear.

You must read the Word of God every day and store its truths in your heart, so that you carry it with you wherever you go. This is crucial to being established in his love for you. Like nothing else, the Bible reveals the heart of this God we have been invited to know. To neglect reading it in any part is to neglect some part of what God has chosen to reveal to you about Himself.

Third, take God's promises out for a spin.

Let me be frank: even after my initial and wonderful experience of God's love, God was on trial with me in those early months, as I think he is with most new believers. So as I read my Bible, I tested his words, by obeying them.

God proved to me that obeying Him always increased my experience of his love, even if I didn't understand at the beginning how it would. God passed all of my tests, and it became settled in my heart and mind: I could trust God's character, his motives, and his love for me. I could trust his Words to give me more life as I believed in and acted upon them.

After God passed my tests, obedience came easier, because I didn't have to stop and wrestle with God on every little issue. It is much easier to yield wholeheartedly to God when you are absolutely convinced that his primary motive is to love you completely and bring you into his abundant life. The Hebrews had the Promised Land, and we have our Promised Life. The stories of their struggles and what God says about the Promised

Land are all shadows of truth and lessons to be learned about our Promised Life with God — yet another reason to be sure you read all of the Old Testament as well as the New.

Fourth, respond to the Holy Spirit.

Once I understood my need to be filled with the Holy Spirit, I learned to live in the awareness of his presence. Never forget the Holy Spirit is a person, the personal presence of God. Don't ignore Him, grieve Him, or expose Him to unholy things. Live in the awareness that he is right with you, sees what you see, hears what you hear, knows your every thought, feeling, and need.

In this awareness you can cultivate the intimate relationship with God as you would anyone, with one difference: in this relationship, there is unlimited potential. In other words, you can fully trust this person, without fear. You are not constrained by circumstances or time because the Holy Spirit is always with you, ready to comfort, guide, teach, and empower you, to continually confirm that you are God's child. In short, learn to live your life as a response to the presence of the Lord, the Holy Spirit.

> **Learn to live your life as a response to the presence of the Lord, the Holy Spirit.**

Finally, obey the Lord trustfully.

I learned by experience that trusting Him — showed by obedience — firmly establishes you in his love. Obedience throws you upon Him entirely, where you must trust in and test his goodness. Only through obedience will you discover the depth and height and width and length of God's love —

the very thing Paul prayed for you in Ephesians 3. Jesus agrees. The night before he went to the cross, he said to his disciples:

> *"As the Father has loved me, so have I loved you. Now remain in my love. If you obey my commands, you will remain in my love, just as I have obeyed my Father's commands and remain in his love." (John 15:9-10).*

"Now remain in my love." How? "Obey my commands."

If God is love, and Jesus came to give us life more abundant, then any command he gives us (by the Holy Spirit or by Scripture) can only be an expression of that love. The one who yields to God's will finds himself walking a personal path paved by God's love, always coming from one experience of being loved and on the way to the next. When you believe that God's love is contained in every command he gives, you will always have a "yes" in your heart for Him.

It is true, in obedience you may lose things you presently value, and there will be times when obeying God is such a sacrifice that it hurts; but the testimony of countless believers is that God always rewards with his obedient ones with more than he has taken away. He said as much in Mark 10:29-30:

> *"I tell you the truth," Jesus replied, "no one who has left home or brothers or sisters or mother or father or children or fields for me and the gospel will fail to receive a hundred times as much in this present age (homes, brothers, sisters, mothers, children and fields — and with them, persecutions) and in the age to come, eternal life."*

Peter Lord says it like this: "With God you always trade up."

I do not want to sugar coat the truth: there have been times when obeying God caused me to sincerely grieve for a season; yet without exception God comforted me deeply in that grief with his peace and often even a surprising joy in it —

what I can only describe as God allowing me to share his pleasure in my act of love for Him. And the greater life that always comes to me later makes any suffering similar to what I experienced in giving birth to my children: temporary, bearable, forgotten in the joy that followed.

> "Now remain in my love."
> How?
> "Obey my commands."

This is my testimony: the longer I walk with God the more it is reinforced that God richly rewards. He abundantly loves. He lavishly cares for us. But we only experience this love by way of obedience. That is the meaning of 1 John 2:5:

> But if anyone obeys his word, God's love is truly made complete in him.

When I obey God, I am letting Him love me best.

The purpose of faith is to believe in God's presence and his love. This is the means by which He transforms and satisfies the hungry heart. Don't settle for anything less than experiencing his love and learning to love in response. The world is already full of "faith" people who have not entered the life of love, who have not shown God to the world, nor been transformed in character and life. (If you are in the midst of such a people, don't judge them or preach at them, just become established in God's love yourself, and become salt to make them thirsty.)

I had read the above verse in 1 John for years before I noticed a footnoted, alternate translation in the NIV that reads:

> But if anyone obeys his words, love for God is truly made complete in him.

This is a perfect example of something I have noticed more and more through years of reading the Word of God: that many verses are like a double-edged sword, having more than one meaning or application. It preaches both ways: obeying God's word makes his love for us complete, and it makes our love for God complete, fully expressed and realized.

The bottom line: becoming established in love is a process of relationship between two people that happens through a season of shared experiences. That's why we were given the Holy Spirit, so we could experience the love of God, the thoughts of God, and the comforting voice of God. The Lord dwells in the secret place of your heart and spirit. No book, no teacher, no other individual can discover for us what God's love demands that we find for ourselves.

Your experience will not be like mine. God has a wonderful, unique and personal way of revealing his love to his children. So don't try to seek my wave of love. Invite God to come and reveal his love to you in the way that is just right for you. When your prayer is answered, you will know that the Holy Spirit has come and enabled you to experience the love of the Father and of Jesus the Son. It is what you were made for, and how you were meant to live.

Why Is Loving God So Hard For Us?

It would be unfair to write to you of being established in the love life without acknowledging the common difficulties we face in trying to do so. While God has provided everything we need through the Holy Spirit to enter this life with Him, stepping into that provision is certainly not an automatic or uniform experience — because we humans are, well, human. Some things we need to realize about the obstacles presented by our humanness are discussed here.

Only a circumcised heart can love God

First of all, God must circumcise our hearts to enable us love Him, as he taught through Moses centuries ago:

> *The Lord your God will circumcise your hearts and the hearts of your descendants, so that you may love Him with all your heart and with all your soul, and live. (Deuteronomy 30:6)*

If you're like I was in my Christian infancy, you are curiously wondering, just how and when does God do this circumcision? We find some clues in Colossians, where Paul spoke of it in connection with being baptized in water:

> *In him you were also circumcised, in the putting off of the sinful nature, not with a circumcision done by the hands of men but with the circumcision done by Christ,*

> *having been buried with him in baptism and raised with him through your faith in the power of God, who raised him from the dead. When you were dead in your sins and in the uncircumcision of your sinful nature, God made you alive with Christ. He forgave us all our sins... Colossians 2:11-13*

If you have read our materials on Covenant, you already know the importance of water baptism. Jesus said we should be baptized, and doing so is our first act of obedience as we come to Christ. He clearly instructed his disciples to baptise those they brought into the faith. We don't know everything that happens in water baptism, but we do know it is important to the Lord. If there is indeed a connection between water baptism and the moment God normally circumcises the human heart of its sinful flesh nature, then the absence of obedience to this baptism might be a reason why one has trouble loving God.

In many years of ministry we've met a significant number of Christians who continued to struggle with sin, who had never been baptized in water. At the very least we consider water baptism essential to beginning a healthy covenant life with the Lord where we show our willingness to humble ourselves and obey just as our brother Jesus did. In fact, considering that the son of God submitted to public baptism, how much more should we do the same, as he said, *"to fulfill all righteousness!"* (That's just a fancy term for, "It's the right thing to do.")

We just don't really believe what God says.

Another reason we may have trouble loving God is that, quite frankly, we just don't believe Him. We can believe IN Him and still not believe what he tells us about Himself and how he wants to relate to us. The greatest work of faith is to simply take God at his Word and adjust our lives, thoughts and attitudes accordingly.

> The greatest work of faith is to simply take God at his Word and adjust our lives, thoughts and attitudes accordingly.

We don't know this invisible God very well, but we really have no excuse because he has revealed Himself in the Bible. We should read every word of it, thus showing value for the greatest privilege of our covenant: the privilege of knowing God. Something about his heart is revealed on nearly every page; to have no interest in reading and understanding the Bible is tantamount to having little interest in knowing God. And all that stuff about worshiping and adoring Him isn't referring to something you are just supposed to force yourself to do as one of those Christian rules; worship and adoration are meant to be the natural response to experiencing who God really is and what He has actually done for us. Not believing what God has said about Himself makes it much harder to love Him.

We don't believe God satisfies

Many find it hard to seek after and love God because they don't really believe God has the ability to satisfy them. They know God is eventually going to take them to heaven, and most believe He will meet their basic needs and get them out of hot water. Others who have a deeper faith may easily believe God will provide for them financially, heal their bodies, and do other miraculous things, but even many of these folks don't honestly believe that God can actually satisfy the deepest needs of the heart — for things like contentment, understanding, justice, connection. Yet it is turning to God with all your need — and having Him respond — that will cause your love for Him to grow. I have a story to tell you about how I learned firsthand how much God can satisfy the heart.

I smoked for 18 years, and enjoyed every cigarette I smoked. The Lord actually tolerated my smoking for a few years after I became a Christian, then finally put his foot down one day. I'm quite sure he hoped I would make the decision on my own, and seemingly he had more pressing issues he wanted to work on in getting me to become more like his Son. But one day he said, "It's time. I want you to lay down those cigarettes."

Of course, I had tried many times to stop smoking all those years, out of concern for my health, the smell, the expense, the shame of being a pastor's wife with an addiction — but was too weak to make myself stick with it. Clearly none of these was a strong enough motivation for me. Now I had an entirely different reason to quit: God was calling time. Still, all I could think of was how often I had tried and failed to quit. Then the Lord asked me to think about all of the reasons why I lit up, which took the focus off of my failure to quit and put it on all of my motivation to keep smoking.

As I did this I saw that when I was unhappy, I smoked a cigarette. When I was excited, I smoked a cigarette. When I was working and completed a task I tended to reward myself with a cigarette, and when I just wanted to relax, I smoked a cigarette. I used cigarettes to sooth feelings, to calm me down, to satisfy cravings for other things (like dessert when I was trying to diet). Clearly, I was celebrating all the moments of my life with a cigarette. The Lord then said to me, "I want to be the one you to turn to satisfy your needs and celebrate your little moments of life."

I wanted very much to be found faithful in loving God. By asking me to lay down my cigarettes and give Him the opportunity to satisfy my heart, he had made it personal, much more personal than if he just said, "I's time to quit." It just so happened that I'd been noticing about that same time several scriptures which talked about how God wants to satisfy us, such as Psalm 145:16:

"You open your hand and satisfy the desires of every living thing."

As I thought of those, I was challenged: did I really believe Him?

I thought to myself, All right, this is either true, or it is not, and there is only one way to find out. I laid down the cigarettes. It was not easy, but with God's help, I did it, and in the process I was delighted to discover that God does have the ability to satisfy a heart, when given the opportunity, and that in itself grew my love for Him. If you are afraid to hope that God can and will really satisfy your heart, loving Him will be more of a challenge.

> **If you are afraid to hope that God can and will really satisfy your heart, loving Him will be more of a challenge.**

We don't realize we are helpless to do it on our own

Some Christians are never rooted in love because they were strong, self-sufficient, successful individuals to begin with. They may be well-educated and trained, perhaps managers in the business world, or just used to being in control. These tend to take charge of their own spiritual growth instead of relying upon the help they need from the Spirit of Christ.

It will be difficult for a person like this until he or she realizes how utterly helpless they are apart from the help of the Holy Spirit. It is often the weak person, the simple or childlike one, who is totally spiritually bankrupt (and knows it), that is more easily rooted in loving God. They know just how much help they need. Perhaps that is one reason Jesus said that unless we become like little children — naturally humble in and unashamed of our lack of knowledge and sophistication — we could not enter the Kingdom of heaven. Think of it: our greatest asset in view of achieving our place in God's kingdom is.... childlikeness.

We're afraid love will cost us something

Unquestionably, loving God and other people will cost you something; and there is no doubt that choosing to love may cause us to suffer or make sacrifices. No one likes to suffer, and sacrifice comes easy for no one. All I can tell you is that God has healed every place I have suffered for choosing to love, and rewarded me for every sacrifice. He has been so consistent in this that I have lost my fear of being hurt or being impoverished by love. Yes, love will cost you, but it will give you back so much more — especially when God is on the other end of the equation.

Why Love Is The Greatest Commandment

What is it about love that makes it so important? Honestly, most rulers would tend to rely on sheer power or intimidation or wealth to make their kingdoms secure; but not our God! Furthermore, God could have easily put forth something like staying free of sin as being the most important command to keep. But no, he went for love. True, he is not speaking of the *emotion* of love, he means the *commitment* to love.

How different things would be if love were a gift simply bestowed on you, like healing, words of knowledge or miracles; we would all love much more! But love is a fruit, something that only develops when a parent/host plant is unhindered in expressing its created design. In our case that parent/host is the Holy Spirit, and the fruit of committed love comes only as He is free to express God's design for life in and through our hearts and mind. There is no other way to develop love but through relationship and time.

In First Corinthians 13, Paul says some astounding things about love, in regards to its place, power and purpose in the kingdom of God. First, he assures us that love is greater than all the powerful miracle gifts enabled by the Holy Spirit:

> *"If I speak in the tongues of men and of angels, but have not love, I am only a resounding gong or a clanging cymbal. If I have the gift of prophecy and can fathom all mysteries and all knowledge, and if I have a faith that can move mountains, but have not love, I am nothing. If*

I give all I possess to the poor and surrender my body to the flames, but have not love, I gain nothing." verses 1-3

So much for amazing power and giftedness being the main thing. According to Paul, speaking in tongues without love in your heart is useless; giving prophecies in the absence of love is spiritual showmanship; mountain-moving faith does not impress heaven if you do not love. In fact, sacrificing everything — even to the point of dying for Christ — is wasted on God if it is not motivated by extravagant love.

Love always protects, trusts, hopes, and perseveres

Anyone who has loved deeply knows that love has an unmatched power to keep a relationship strong and draw out the good in a human heart. Paul described it like this:

"[Love] always protects, always trusts, always hopes, always perseveres." verse 7

Consider the love of God: when you have faith in God's love it is easier to trust Him, because no matter what happens, you believe God's motives towards you are always good ones. As I came to faith in God's love, I reasoned that if God is love, then his will is always going to be a faithful expression of that love. Whatever he gives or commands will be an expression of his love; whatever he permits will never make a lie of his love.

When you are rooted in God's love, unpleasant circumstances won't cause you

> **When you don't completely understand what is going on, love will carry you where disciplined faith cannot.**

to abandon your hope in Him. You can persevere with Him, still taking comfort from his faithful love through the storms of life even when you don't completely understand what is going on. Love will carry you where disciplined faith cannot.

Loving God is more important than following the rules

I once saw a t-shirt on a teenager which read, *"No rules."* On the back it said, *"Rules are for people who don't know what to do."* I imagine he wore it to be cheeky, but God used it to make me aware of the vast difference between relationships governed by rules and those governed by love. Love teaches us naturally what to do. Genuine love for another guides and teaches you how to treat them; we can all attest to this in our own lives.

Think about this in relation to your family: children, as long as you show love to your parents by obeying them and displaying respect, there is a closeness between you. They rarely have to drag out the rules and make an issue of them. This is true of any relationship. The primary reason God gave his people the Ten Commandments is because they did not know how to love Him or one another. Rules are only for those who don't know what to do. Those who do not love need something to show them how to govern their behavior while the ability to love is still coming to maturity.

There is a consistent thread in the Bible of those who enjoyed a relationship with God outside of the rules — men like Moses and David — and it was always for the same reason: God always honored their passion to know and love Him. God says, "I will be found by those who seek me."

When you love someone, you don't need a script in order to talk to them. Did anyone have to tell you how to talk to the beloved people in your life? Of course not! That's why, as we mature in love for God, we should move beyond our reliance upon prayers composed by others. Do learn what you can about the art of prayer; but once you come to a place of genuine love for the Lord, you shouldn't need anyone to tell you how to talk to God, because your heart will teach you. And by the way, when you talk to God, do it as if he is right there — because he is.

Moses, David, Paul and others in the Bible learned how to relate to God in wonderful, intimate ways without the benefit of Bibles, cd's, dvd's or conferences. They were hungry to know God Himself, and ever faithful to his promise, God responded to that hunger by revealing Himself to them. As a result, love for Him grew, which is the inevitable result of getting to know and experience this amazing God of ours.

> You were never meant to drum up love or talk yourself into feeling it, but to live as a witness to his goodness and experience the deep satisfaction of knowing Him.

The one thing God wants the most, his power cannot produce for Him: passionate lovers captivated by his beauty and majesty, hungry for all of who he is and what he wants to share out of his goodness. You were never meant to drum up love or talk yourself into feeling it. You were meant to live as a witness to his goodness, to experience the deep satisfaction of knowing Him — much like human love, which is a type and shadow of divine love.

We will do things for love we wouldn't do for any other reason.

I can best make this point by sharing a personal story. I ended up marrying that fine preacher two years after I joined the church. We did pretty well the first couple of years, especially since we were trying to blend two families, but by the third year, our marriage was in serious trouble. (I share this story in detail in my book <u>The Woman God Designed</u>.)

Amazingly, we were two Christians who sincerely wanted to do things God's way, a pastor who was very good at counseling others, and a pastor's wife skillfully teaching the Bible, especially to women. We prayed and read our Bibles faithfully. We really did love God, and we loved each other, yet our marriage was failing, and we were hurting one other more deeply than we had imagined possible as we increasingly fell into heated and divisive arguments.

One day in the midst of a vicious argument I realized I felt real hatred towards Ron, and I could see it coming back at me in his eyes. The moment I saw that, I was done. I ran out of the house just to get away from him, while he shouted after me, "Good, don't ever come back!" I could not imagine any relationship more hopeless than ours at that moment.

I drove off, but I was crying so hard that I had to pull into a grocery store parking lot, where I cried out to God about all my hurt, and raged against my husband. The Lord was quiet as I begged Him not to make me go back to Ron. Surely, I thought, he would not make me stay in such a broken, painful relationship. I was convinced that divorce was the only possible end to this situation, but I had no idea what to do or where to go. Finally I quieted down and asked, *"Lord, what do you want me to do?"* The answer came: *"Toni, if you love me, go home to your husband."*

Not, If you love your husband, or You know I hate divorce, or You know divorce is a sin, but, If you love me…

God, it seems, is a master at re-framing the moment and the issue. Suddenly the issue wasn't the state of my marriage, it was about me and God.

Of course, as usual I'd been set up beforehand by the Holy Spirit, who had me reading in the gospel of John for weeks. I practically knew it by heart at this point, and very fresh in my mind were the words from John chapter 14 where Jesus says, *"If you love me, you will obey me."* (In fact, He says this three times, and in case you still don't get it after all that repetition, He says it in reverse: *"Those who do not obey me are not my disciples; they do not love me!"*)

My thoughts raced in two directions: on one hand, going back to Ron was unthinkable, resigning myself to a life of misery and pain. I couldn't bear the thought of it. On the other hand, if I didn't obey what the Lord had just asked of me, my actions would say that I did not love Him. I could tell others I loved God and get away with it, but I could not go to the secret, precious place with God again and say, "I love you, Lord" with a clear conscience. I sat there and weighed it all in my heart and mind. It was the hardest decision I had ever faced.

Something else was bothering me as well: the thought that if I left Ron, I would shame God's name in our church and community. I had been teaching in Sunday School that you can do anything with the help of Christ. I thought of how my students would lose faith in Jesus if they saw our marriage fall apart. In that moment, I experienced the way that love wants to protect, because I wanted to protect Jesus' reputation and couldn't bear to let Him down in that way.

Finally there was one other, very important truth rolling around in there with all my other thoughts: that Jesus said he came to give us abundant life. That was the very first moment when it occurred to me that if this was really true, then in spite of how it all looked, whatever the Lord asked me to do would be in keeping with that promise. It just couldn't be otherwise. I decided to go home.

Here's what I want you to get from this story: I didn't go home because I was a strong Christian, or because I was righteous, or because I loved my husband. I had absolutely no confidence in my husband or myself to change; I didn't even have faith that the Lord would somehow change either one of us or the marriage. I went home because I loved Jesus too much to say no, because I couldn't bear to shame his name, and because whatever else was wrong with me and my marriage, I trusted God with all my heart. My desire to love Jesus well, in truth and by my actions, won over my desire to protect myself and go for my own happiness (as I had always done before).

When I got home Ron met me at the door. He had had a similar experience with the Lord! It wasn't a love scene, and there was no tenderness between us. For Jesus' sake we simply surrendered and agreed to try one more time. I am thrilled to report that in time — and actually not nearly as long as one might think — the Lord helped us learned to love one another in the right way. Today we are so grateful.

The Lord has never failed in his promise to give me abundant life. Mine is not a life without problems, but as I write this, 27 years after that parking lot moment of decision, I am more convinced than ever that the Lord is good, and that his love never fails for those who choose to trust in it. As the word says, perfect love casts out fear; in fact, "faith confessions" are far less effective for overcoming fear than absolute confidence in the unfailing love of God. This is also why love is even greater than faith, because love leads us to places where our faith may yet be too weak to take us.

As we leave this story I want to remind you that Jesus would not allow me to make my husband's behavior the issue, nor my own personal feelings and failures. The only issue — which he brought out in stark relief from all the others swirling about — was how would I respond to Him? For a Christian, Jesus is always the issue.

> **I am more convinced than ever that the Lord is good, and that his love never fails for those who choose to trust in it.**

Love carries you through the hard places of obedience.

There have been other times in life I have faced excruciatingly painful choices: to obey God, and thereby open myself to the possibility of emotional pain or great sacrifice, or to say no to God. I am not a strong person; I am weak in many ways. My faith is often not that strong, in myself, in others, or in believing for a good outcome in a situation. But in stark contrast to these weaknesses is my confidence in God's love for me, and my commitment to love Him in truth. Obeying Him always confirms that I can trust Him. He promises we will never face more than we can bear, and I know that his love for me — and you — governs every decision.

Still, in all honesty I must confess that I have failed at times; I have said "No" to the Lord, and instead of loving Him I have made choices based in fear or selfishness. I have at times lost sight of all the things I just said to you. Without exception, I have always regretted these choices, for they always cost me something dear; but I have never once regretted saying yes to God and abandoning myself to love, however risky it may have looked at the moment.

When you say yes to God in an impossible thing, you enter a secret place with Him which no other can enter. It is a secret love place. It is exclusively yours, for it is a place secured by what no other person can give God for you. Only you can give this gift to Him, this gift of yourself, of laying down your life to let Him live his through you.

Love never fails, even in the garden of Gethsemane

These experiences have been for me a small taste of Jesus' agony in the garden of Gethsemane — a very small taste — but sufficient for me to grasp what it's like to agonize over surrender in the face of potential suffering. Consider Jesus, his soul overwhelmed with sorrow; spiritual ambition didn't cause Him to go through with his sacrifice. The terrible knowledge of what he would suffer caused Him so much anguish that his flesh sweat drops of blood. I don't believe that the fact that it was the right thing to do motivated Jesus to surrender to the cross. I'm convinced it was his love for his father, and his love for us.

Love nailed Jesus to a cross long before the soldiers arrived with their hammers.

Love is the greatest motivator there is. You will do things for love that you will not do for any other reason. Parents know this from taking care of their children, especially in the messy, helpless years, the years of sleepless nights and countless dirty diapers and relentless inconveniences. Ask anyone who has sacrificed much of their own life to care for an elderly parent or a handicapped relative.

You will do things for love you would not or could not do for any other reason, which is one primary reason why love is the greatest commandment governing our relationship to God.

We must not forget that Jesus not only loved us on the cross, he loved us all the way to the cross. John 13:1 says,

> *It was just before the Passover Feast. Jesus knew that the time had come for him to leave this world and go to the Father. Having loved his own who were in the world, he now showed them the full extent of his love.*

Having loved his own... this is a past tense expression. You see, if Jesus had sinned even once, he could not have gone to the cross. Jesus loved us all the way to the cross, every day of his life, each time he refused to give in to sin or selfish ambition. The Bible says he was tempted to sin in every way that humans are, yet he was able to say no. This means that while living as a man just like us, Jesus experienced what it is like to be us, in all the vulnerability of emotion and desire and will.

I believe when Jesus said "no" to sin it wasn't just because he had a strong will, but because he loved the Father (and us) too much to do otherwise. While the cross was the supreme expression of his love, it was also the consummation of years of loving us with all his might! Every time Jesus said no to sin, it was an act of love for his father and for us. If He had committed one sin, had given into temptation even once, the cross would never have been possible, and we would be lost forever.

That monumental moment of sacrificial love could not have happened without all the lesser moments that led up to it.

Jesus made his choices motivated by love. Was he just born loving like this because he was the Son of God? I don't think so. I believe Jesus was able to love with all strength because he himself had been rooted and established in the Father's love. And that came about for him, as a human being, in the same way it will for us: through the ministry of the Holy Spirit, helping us to experience the Father's love, and guiding us in how to love the Father.

Between the bookends of love we are transformed

Love is the greatest command because love is what transforms us: first his love for us, then our love for Him. God's love for us begins the transformation, because at first we are so thankful to be forgiven, accepted and loved as we need, that we are willing to change. As I came to know God more, I understood that what he wanted most from me was my heart, entrusted to his care through acts of obedience. Then the blessings I experienced through obedience made me love Him more. The more I love Him the more I am committed to obediently surrender to his will, and these choices took me to deeper levels of transformation, a process that is ongoing. Without a doubt, I am a different woman today, a transformation achieved somewhere between the bookends of being loved by God and loving Him back. I now know that change in character is not something you can just make yourself do. You cannot make yourself be a different person. I tried, and failed. But while I was busy loving God, He changed me.

> Love is the greatest command because love is what transforms us: first his love for us, then our love for Him.

Love covers many sins and takes us past ourselves

Remember the sinful woman who so boldly approached Jesus in the house of the (self-)righteous Pharisees? She loved Jesus so much that she brought a precious perfume — worth a year's wages — to pour on Him in an extravagant act of worship:

> *Now one of the Pharisees invited Jesus to have dinner with him, so he went to the Pharisee's house and reclined at the table. When a woman who had lived a sinful life in that town learned that Jesus was eating at the Pharisee's house, she brought an alabaster jar of perfume, and as she stood behind him at his feet weeping, she began to wet his feet with her tears. Then she wiped them with her hair, kissed them and poured perfume on them. When the Pharisee who had invited him saw this, he said to himself, "If this man were a prophet, he would know who is touching him and what kind of woman she is — that she is a sinner." Luke 7:36-39*

In Jesus' day any self-respecting "holy" man would never allow a sinful woman to touch Him; nor would such a woman dare to walk a gauntlet of judgmental Pharisees to carry out the most tender, extravagant — and frankly inappropriate — act of love and worship for one who was as pure as she had been sinful. But this woman, her love flowing out in a river of tears, washed Jesus' feet with that love and that precious perfume.

This woman's love for Jesus overtook her fear of what others thought of her. Her desire to bless Him and serve Him in some way carried her past all self-consciousness about her sinful life. Jesus had not just convinced her to leave that sinful life; he had inspired a love in her that wiped out (or rendered irrelevant) how she saw herself. Her love for Him — and her confidence in his love for her — removed any fear that he would rebuke her or turn an indifferent cheek; it destroyed every barrier between them, whether those barriers were self-consciousness, social or religious tradition, fear, or station in life.

In the midst of a bunch of rule-followers, she broke every cultural rule, and probably some of their religious laws; yet she fulfilled the law of love, which made her in that moment, next to Jesus, the most righteous soul in the room. This is the power of love: to change our behavior, our mindset, our view of ourselves, others and the world. Love changed her very identity.

And in the matter of approaching a holy god, love covers a multitude of sins:

> *Jesus answered him, "Simon, I have something to tell you." "Tell me, teacher," he said. "Two men owed money to a certain money-lender. One owed him five hundred denarii, and the other fifty. Neither of them had the money to pay him back, so he cancelled the debts of both. Now which of them will love him more?" Simon replied, "I suppose the one who had the bigger debt cancelled." "You have judged correctly," Jesus said.*
>
> *Then he turned towards the woman and said to Simon, "Do you see this woman? I came into your house. You did not give me any water for my feet, but she wet my feet with her tears and wiped them with her hair. You did not give me a kiss, but this woman, from the time I entered, has not stopped kissing my feet. You did not put oil on my head, but she has poured perfume on my feet. Therefore, I tell you, her many sins have been forgiven — for she loved much. But he who has been forgiven little loves little."*
>
> *Then Jesus said to her, "Your sins are forgiven." The other guests began to say among themselves, "Who is this who even forgives sins?" Jesus said to the woman, "Your faith has saved you; go in peace." Luke 7:40-50*

Here's what I wonder when I read the last two verses: what faith was Jesus referring to? What did she have faith in, that saved her?

I think it was faith in the character of Christ; faith that who HE is, is more important than who she had been. This woman was transformed by her faith in the unfailing love of Jesus Christ. Somehow she grasped in simple relational terms what God took much trouble to demonstrate in the Ark of the Covenant: that the law — that perfect expression of who God is (and how we should be) — is covered by the mercy seat (what you now know is *chesed,* unfailing love) of God. This scene in Jesus' life is perfect theology and right doctrine in a simple, beautiful act of love.

Love delivers us from self

In the absence of love for God, the eyes are always on self, what we call self-consciousness. There is pride (protecting self's image of itself) and fear (what is going to happen that will hurt self); there is record-keeping: you did this to me (self).

There has been much talk in the Body of Christ about "dying to self," and indeed, I have been one of those who strenuously tried to do just that. But I learned that focusing on dying to self actually keeps self very much alive and in focus. The Lord has taught me finally that dying to self is not something you set out to do. What you set out to do is love others so well that you forget yourself. In other words, self dies while you're not looking.

Love purifies our hearts. We all need to be purified, to be cleansed of that which soils our souls, which mars

> **Dying to self is not something you set out to do. When you set out to love others well, you forget yourself, and self dies while you're not looking.**

the beauty God created us to display in his image. Purification can be achieved in several ways, such as judgment, discipline, hardship and punishment. Everyone ever spanked by a parent knows how effective that can be to get us to stop doing wrong behavior. But by far, God's number one choice for purification, is love. When we are committed to love, love itself purifies our heart.

The choice is yours, but the Apostle Paul recommends the way of love:

> *And this is my prayer: that your love may abound more and more... so that you ... may be pure and blameless until the day of Christ...."* [Philippians 1:9-11]

Love is the only source of true worship

He knows when worship is sincere and when it is for public show, or a bow to peer pressure. The true heart that demonstrates love for God in community worship also sings to Him when no one else is watching. Love dances with joy before the Lord in its own living room, or during sunrise solitude in the garden. This is the kind of worshiper the Father is looking for, one who worships in spirit and in truth.

God's throne is established through love

When my heart filled with real affection for Him, Jesus had a much easier time ruling my heart. I then understood why Proverbs 20:28 says of a ruler, *"through love his throne is made secure."* A kingdom made up of devoted, loving servants is far more secure than a kingdom made up of reluctant slaves.

Christ can reign in your heart far better when you love Him. If he only rules your heart because you have set your human will on being a good servant, you will only go so far; you will be likely to falter in the difficult moments. When teaching his disciples about the end of time, Jesus warned: *"Be-*

cause of the increase of wickedness, the love of most will grow cold, but he who stands firm to the end will be saved." In saying this Jesus clearly linked love with the kind of salvation that endures to the end.

How sad to know that many who are saved (actually Jesus used the word "most") could possibly throw their salvation away at the end because they don't sincerely love God. I am not saying that a person doesn't go to heaven if he doesn't love Jesus the right way; I'm just repeating what Jesus said: the person who is not motivated by and empowered (through the Holy Spirit) to love, may abandon Christ and his own faith when really difficult times come.

As we approach the second coming of Jesus Christ we can be certain times will grow darker and evil will increase; we have his word on it. We must be those who love Christ with all our might, and we must learn how to do that now before the going gets really tough. If you have not learned to love God, if you have not sought the help of the Holy Spirit to help you in this, you could abandon Christ more easily than you might think. In these times, I think there is no more important "end times ministry" than that of teaching people to be firmly established in the love of God.

How Do I Love God Like This?

> *Love the Lord your God with all your heart and with all your soul and with all your mind and with all your strength. Mark 12:30*

Love God with all your soul. The Greek word used here for soul is *psuche*, which refers to all that distinguishes one human being from another: one's thoughts, desires, and feelings — the sum of one's personality.

In light of the words of Mark 12:30, consider your own soul. Would you say that you love God with the thoughts you allow to live in your mind, in that place where no one goes but you and God? What about your feelings such as anger, disappointment, or fear, your habitual emotional responses to people and situations? Do you believe you have been actively loving God with your will — the choices you make, the things you desire, the goals you work towards? Every part of who we are should be actively expressing love for God.

Jesus said to the religious leaders of his day, *"Isaiah was right when he prophesied about you hypocrites; as it is written: 'These people honor me with their lips, but their hearts are far from me.'"* (Mark 7:6). In other words, outwardly they looked and sounded like they cared about God, but in the secret place of their thoughts and emotions, they were nowhere near his heart.

Loving God with your thoughts

If we would honor the greatest commandment, we should be actively loving God in the secret place of our thoughts, where no one knows what they are except us and God. To love God with your mind is to see it as a place that is holy — i.e., set apart exclusively — for God's use. The mind of man was made to be a place where God would abide and be at home in, a place from which to allow you to reveal his glory and creativity, and to communicate his goodness to the world. It was not meant to be a place of brooding on how to get even with those who hurt you, nor a storeroom for the offenses and trespasses of others. Neither was it intended to be a nursery for self-pity or a fortress of fear or torment in the form of regrets, pressure, self-reproach or anxiety.

Your mind is a gift from God, the likes of which has been given to no other creature. The Bible says that God knows the thoughts of a man. Is He loved in them? Or is he doubted, or perhaps even despised? In your secret thoughts, do you accuse God of evil? If you do not love God with your mind, no one else may discover it, but God knows.

If thoughts of lust arise, to love God would be to turn away from those thoughts and give them no room to dwell. To love God is to see such thoughts, not as part of yourself, but as an enemy to be captured and put out. Paul teaches this in 2 Corinthians 10:5 when he says:

> *We demolish arguments and every pretension that sets itself up against the knowledge of God, and we take captive every thought to make it obedient to Christ.*

The Bible teaches that when we become a child of God we are to be "renewed" in our minds. That means to let God change your mind; to let Him tell you what to think and how to make right judgments about people and situations. To love God with all your soul is to love his truth and values as your own.

Practically speaking, this means two things. First, we should read God's Word to learn what he values, then be willing to exchange our values for his where we see they are different. God's judgment of what is good or evil should become our attitude towards those things. If we see that he values humility and faithfulness, then we should value those things more than some celebrity's lifestyle and personna.

Second, in prayer, as we listen for God's counsel, we should invite the Holy Spirit to weigh in on what we think and believe. One's belief system is incredibly important, because what you believe becomes the source of all that you come to feel or desire, the choices you make, and how you choose to behave. For example, let's say you have formed an opinion or judgment about someone; it is good to say to God, "What do you think about how I think of them?"

This is the first step towards also loving God in your emotions. The reason for that is that feelings are not inherently right or wrong by their nature, since anger, jealousy and hatred are not wrong under the right circumstances (even God feels these things in their proper time).

When you form an opinion or judgment about someone, it is good to ask God, "What do you think about how I think of them?"

Loving God with your emotions

It seems at first glance that we cannot help feeling what we feel, but actually all feelings are born in us as a response to what is believed about what we see or experience. People often wrestle with feelings and attitudes that they know aren't right (such as unforgiveness) as if they should just be able to make themselves NOT feel what they feel. But that is the hard way to go about it.

Two things can change your feelings. The first is discovering if your perception, or what you believe about the person or situation, is accurate. Is the judgment you have made based on accuracy, on truth? Do you know all the facts? If not, your feelings may be completely unfounded and unnecessary.

The second thing that can change your feelings — especially for a Christian — is to ask (and answer) the question: *"What is the right(eous) response to what I know?"*

Again, in order to love God with your emotions you need to take your beliefs, opinions and judgments to God and ask, "What do you think about this?" or "What do you think of my response to this?" Let God weigh in; seek his truth. This is what scripture is referring to when it speaks of "walking in the light" — meaning to let God shine a line on the dark corners of your heart and mind and make things clear to you. Asking Him to do this his honors Him, which is another great way to love Him.

This gives God the opportunity to counsel you in the place where emotions are born, to help you know if those emotions are appropriate or not. James 1:5-6 says,

If any of you lacks wisdom, he should ask God, who gives generously to all without finding fault, and it will be given to him. But when he asks, he must believe and not doubt...

God is generous with his wisdom, and loves to provide it to the child who honors Him by asking, and has faith that he will answer. So when you ask, pay immediate attention to the words, thoughts, pictures or emotional impressions that come. God speaks to us in all these ways, as well as speaking to us through scripture.

Sometimes I form an opinion or a judgment about someone or some situation, only to realize that the Lord doesn't agree with me. To love Him with my soul in such a moment is to abandon my opinions and let his truth be my truth, his judgments my judgments. Remember that the religious leaders who brought the adulterous wife to Jesus were quite certain he would have judgment, anger, righteous indignation and hatred for her and her sin, and stone her as the law called for. But Jesus, who said clearly to his followers, *"I do not judge on my own, but only as I hear my Father..."* had an entirely different reaction: he judged the judges, while showing compassion and mercy to the woman. If the Son of God thought it was right to check in with the Father on how to judge and what to feel, how much more should we!

Of course, when it comes to anything you feel that you know is not consistent with loving God — things he hates such as hatred, rage, bitterness or jealousy — you should try get rid of those emotions. Emotions do carry us away, especially if we are very hurt or very angry. Confess wrong thoughts, feelings and judgments to God, and ask Him to cleanse your heart and mind. The Holy Spirit loves to help you with these things.

> **If the Son of God thought it was right to check in with the Father on how to judge and what to feel, how much more should we!**

We must cease to proudly own our feelings as if they are our most treasured possession. We naturally assume our feelings are truth and we have a right to feel them. You will find yourself feeling very possessive of your feelings; you will be reluctant to submit them to the Lord and let Him change them for you. Giving up your feelings seems like giving up yourself, a part of who you are. In essence, this is true, and this is part of the process of dying to self, of laying down your life for love of the Lord. We don't die to self through being invisible wallflowers or and giving someone else the last piece of pecan pie at the fellowship dinner. We die to self when we give up a little bit of what makes us who we are and say goodbye to it forever.

When you love God with all your might and walk in the trust that goes with it, you will not fear letting a little piece of who you are die. Why? Because you will rest in the fact that you don't need that part of who you are. In the act of dying to who you are by nature, you become more like He is by nature. Again, this is the work of the Holy Spirit, and he is always drawing us to it.

Loving God with your desires

Finally, loving God with all of your soul means loving Him with all your will, the very things you desire. Considering the very materialistic and toy-filled culture we live in, it is not always easy to love God in our wants. The world we live in — saturated with slick advertising — continually tries to manipulate us to want what it offers. The more advanced society becomes, the more there is to want, and all that stuff looks good to us.

What does it mean to love God with all your will? First, what it doesn't mean is that you have to give up everything, deny yourself every little desire that rolls across your soul. After all, if God lives in you, then you need to consider that he can be a source of some desires that stir in you. What it does mean is that you should abandon any desire which you clearly understand is not consistent with loving God faithfully. It is not necessary or even automatically good for you to give up everything that all the other Christians you know have given up; our faith walk with God is very personal. There are always going to be things that lead others astray that don't affect me at all, and vice-versa.

There was a time when I had to give up sewing and crafting for awhile, because it was becoming something I pursued with more heart than I did God. The Lord opened my eyes to this, and to his jealousy over my heart, so for a season I deliberately put away my desire and my activity concerning those things. After awhile I knew it was okay to let them back into my life, because I had my priorities in order. When it comes to dealing with desires we need to understand what God wants of us, not someone else, and we should not judge others nor allow them to judge us in matters of faith. Paul speaks of this matter clearly in Romans Chapter 14 — which would be wisdom for you to read as you consider what I have written to you.

Everyone struggles with desires that are not good, whether it concerns God or foods or habits that you love but are bad for you. It is not easy to make ourselves not want what we want, and that thing we call "willpower" is for most, a fickle thing. Trying to make ourselves not want something usually only makes us focus on it all the more! It is only when we truly don't want something anymore that we are able to turn away from it for good, and that generally happens because something else comes along that we want MORE — like to not have cancer or not be overweight. It is much easier to abandon one desire for another, better one, than it is to simply try to quit wanting what we want.

So in the matter of your will, it is better to set your affection on God than it is to wrestle with your will. When it is time to make a choice, we should ask: *"Which choice is the one I can love God with?"* The best way to love God with your will is to simply offer it to Him, invite Him to take your desires and destroy them if he wishes, and replace them with what is pleasing to Him. It helps if you remember that if God doesn't want you to have something, there is a very good reason, a decision he has made based on his knowledge, wisdom and love. And if God wants you to have something, it should be good for you; but never let yourself love God's gifts more than God Himself.

To love God with all your will, in the simplest terms, means to love what God wants more than what you want. It is a sacrifice. It is a sacrifice that has always pleased God more than a thousand bullocks or rams.

Few ever love God this way. We know that Jesus loved the Father this way during his time on earth as a man, because he said to his disciples the night before his crucifixion:

> *I will not speak with you much longer, for the prince of this world is coming. He has no hold on me, but the world must learn that I love the Father and that I do exactly what my Father has commanded me. [John 14:30-31]*

It has always struck me as significant that Jesus connected his wholehearted embrace of his Father's will with the fact that the devil had no hold on Him, no place to hook into his heart. It will be no different for us.

Set your heart on the Lord; feed your hunger on the true Bread

Don't just read devotionals, be devoted. Set your heart upon wanting to know Him. Quit feeding your hunger for God with other things, and let your true hunger for life lead you to eat of the true Bread. You do this by reading the Bible diligently, taking time to meditate upon its truths, and spending time sitting with God. When you pray, expect to enjoy God's presence. Take a journal with you, always being ready to write down what he may say to your heart. Show Him by doing these things that you anticipate and value his words and his presence.

Keep your heart attentive to God's wooing

Song of Songs contains a beautiful depiction of the course of love between two people. Not only does it portray the initial passion and consummation of that passion, it also describes the point in a relationship where the beloved becomes too familiar and even a little bored with her lover. The one who thrilled her heart in the beginning becomes an inconvenience when he knocks on her chamber door one night after she has gone to bed. Instead of responding immediately to his knock, she says to herself,

> *I have taken off my robe — must I put it on again? I have washed my feet — must I soil them again? (Song of Solomon 5:3)*

She hesitates a few moments and finally decides to respond, but when she reaches the door her lover has vanished, sent away by her indifference. The beloved goes searching for him. She finally finds him, but along the way she is beat up, bruised and robbed.

How prophetic this picture is of us and Jesus. After the first blush of love, we often settle into a comfortable religious routine where we may become less and less willing to inconvenience ourselves for Him. Our failure to respond to his little urgings may cost us much. Not only do we miss opportunities to experience more of his passionate and precious love, but we are often needlessly robbed and bruised by the enemy of our souls or even by our own choices.

The analogy doesn't stop there, because the story ends with the beloved finding her lover again and when she does, he does not upbraid her, but pours out his love upon her anew. Jesus never turns away the one who returns to Him, but welcomes us with open arms. He longs for you. You need to believe this with all your heart.

A true lover wants to know and be known

Love craves knowledge of the beloved. You want to know what your beloved hates, and what your beloved loves. You want to know his thoughts. In Proverbs 1:23-25, the voice of Wisdom (revealed in the New Testament to be the voice of the Lord) says, *"If you had listened to me, I would have poured out my heart to you and made my thoughts known to you!"*

You see, the Lord wants to reveal Himself to you. That is why God makes it possible for those who enter life with Him through the New Covenant of Jesus to know his thoughts, as Paul shows us in 1 Corinthians 2:9-12 and 16:

> *However, as it is written: "No eye has seen, no ear has heard, no mind has conceived what God has prepared for those who love him" — but God has revealed it to us by his Spirit. The Spirit searches all things, even the deep things of God. For who among men knows the thoughts of a man except the man's spirit within him? In the same way no-one knows the thoughts of God except the Spirit of God. We have not received the spirit of the world but the Spirit who is from God, that we may understand what God has freely given us....we have the mind of Christ.*

Remember I told you that we live in a covenant with God? And that the greatest provision of the New Covenant is the promise that we will know God? God has provided everything we need to know Him through the Holy Spirit. Because of this we have no excuse; we are invited to know God, we are called to know God, and we CAN know God, know his thoughts, know his desires, understand his heart about a matter, know when we please Him, when we grieve Him, and when we give Him joy.

> **In giving us the Holy Spirit, God has provided everything we need to know Him. We have no excuse. We are invited to know God, we are called to know God, and we can know God.**

These are all the things that mark a relationship of love between two hearts: that we live fully aware of the other person and know how our own behavior and choices affect them... and if we truly love them, we choose to behave in the way that reveals and honors that love.

Obey Him

I have already made the case for obedience in several places here, so I won't repeat myself. I will simply say that Jesus taught his first disciples in John 14 that obedience is the only authentic evidence of our love for God. If you need further convincing, read the book of First John.

You can feel affectionate love for God without obeying Him consistently, but it is only when you obey Him consistently that your love has made the journey from emotion to fact.

You Know You Really Love God When:

He is never far from your thoughts, and you cannot think over any decision without wondering what he would think about it.

The idea of his nearness with you through the day is comforting.

You expect to enjoy Him.

You sing to Him, even when you're not in church.

You pray (talk) to Him even when it is not designated prayer time.

You study the Bible when you're not even in Sunday School or church, because you want to know what God is like, what delights Him, what makes Him angry. You want to know what he hates and what he loves, so you can love and hate with Him. You don't read to be a scholar; you read to know the heart of God. You're hungry to discover who He is for yourself rather than cling to a version you've heard somewhere else

You aren't uncomfortable being still and quiet while waiting for Him; you don't feel like you have to make a conversation happen, but you want to always show God the honor of showing up and you're willing to wait.

You keep a journal handy in case he says something you never want to forget.

You love Him whether he blesses you today or not.

You long for Him more than things or healing or anointing or wisdom.

You hate the idea of letting Him down or offending Him.

You would rather receive correction from Him than not hear anything at all.

Disobedience is more uncomfortable to you than obedience.

You want to protect his name, see his glory revealed to the world, and for others to know this amazing, wonderful God.

Conclusion and Prayer

It is important to get rid of any wrong root for your relationship to God, and to be established in an intimate relationship governed by God's love for you and your love for Him. This is one of the most important functions of the Holy Spirit in a Christian's life (since you can't do it without Him) and is a primary reason you need to be filled with the Holy Spirit, as the New Testament makes clear. (More detailed teaching on these issues is available on the audio series "Spirit Life" or "Entering God's Rest," and the other books in this series, available on our website at www.shammah.org.)

Meanwhile, without delay you should ask Jesus to baptise you in the Holy Spirit, and trust Him to do so. According to Galatians 3:1-6, this baptism is received through faith, just like salvation. Ask, believe, and trust the Holy Spirt with your whole heart. After all, He is the Lord. Remember what Paul wrote of Him in his second letter to the Corinthian church:

> *Now the Lord is the Spirit, and where the Spirit of the Lord is, there is freedom. And we, who with unveiled faces all reflect the Lord's glory, are being transformed into his likeness with ever-increasing glory, which comes from the Lord, who is the Spirit. (2 Corinthians 3:17-18)*
>
> *We have this treasure in jars of clay to show that this all-surpassing power is from God and not from us. (2 Corinthians 4:7)*

An example of how to pray:

Dear Lord,

I realize that I have been rooted in _____ and hungry for _____. Please forgive me for giving my needy heart to anyone or anything else but you. I ask you to remove this root and give you permission to do so.

Lord, I offer all of myself to you, including my weakness, my flaws, and my needs. I believe you made me for yourself and that you alone can satisfy every longing of my heart.

Lord Jesus, please baptize me in the Holy Spirit. By your touch let Him come fill me up, and empower me to be established in the Father's love. Let the Holy Spirit reveal your love to me personally, and teach me how to send my roots down deep in that love.

Then let your Spirit empower me to love you completely. Lord, I confess that I don't know how to love you as I should. Please help me to love you with all of my heart, with all my strength, in my private thoughts, through my emotions, and by what I allow myself to desire. Help me to choose and do and live by only those things which express faithful, unfailing love for you.

I ask all these things in Jesus' name, amen.

Meditate often on Paul's prayer in Ephesians 3:16-19:

"...I fall down on my knees and pray to the Father of all the great family of God... that out of his glorious, unlimited resources he will give you the mighty inner strengthening of His Holy Spirit. And I pray that Christ will be more and more at home in your hearts, living within you as you trust in him.

May your roots go down deep into the soil of God's marvelous love; and may you be able to feel and understand, as all God's children should, how long, how wide, how deep, and how high his love really is; and to experience this love for yourselves, though it is so great that you will never see the end of it or fully know or understand it.

And so at last you will be filled up with God himself.
[The Living Bible]

More Resources from Shammah Ministries

Books

- The Woman God Designed: Living the Life He Longs To Give
- Leader's Group Study Guide for The Woman God Designed
- Can I Really Hear God?
- Finding the Heart of God in Every Book of the Bible

Teaching on CD

- Entering God's Rest
- What Kind of Woman Will I Be?
- The Yielded Heart
- Are You Satisfied With God?
- The Tabernacle of Moses: The Pattern for Today's Priesthood

Teaching Series

- Covenant: God's Principles of Committed Love
- Spirit Life: Walking in God's Abundant Life

These and other products, plus free downloadable resources, are available at www.shammah.org.

About the Author

Tonia Woolever is a speaker, counselor, mentor and author. She lives near Fort Worth with her husband, Dr. Ron Woolever, whom she married in 1981. In 1990 they established Shammah Ministries in order to follow their passion to teach the Body of Christ principles of great relationship with God and others. They have done this work full time since retiring from pastoral ministry in 1993. Their particular calling and passion is to reveal the unfailing love of God offered in the New Covenant of Christ, and to help Christians learn how to live as faithful covenant children of God.

In addition to speaking at women's conferences, Tonia often speaks at women's retreats, a favorite setting for her transparent personal style and and her passion to help women to find their rest in God's love. As a counselor and mentor, Tonia helps women learn to hear God for themselves, emphasizing the importance of reading the whole Bible and being filled with and guided by the Holy Spirit. As a teacher to the Body of Christ, Tonia's style is to bring out truths woven throughout the Bible which reveal God's marvelous character, such as the concept that God satisfies his children.

Tonia has many creative loves such as gardening, sewing, knitting, and photography. She finds joy in exuberant worship, good food, great music and movies, plus playing games and laughing with her husband, family and friends.

Tonia & Ron are available individually or as a team for conferences, marriage retreats, leadership training and church seminars. For more information on topics and resources, see their website at: www.shammah.org. If you would like to have Tonia speak at your conference, retreat or other event, email her at tonia@shammah.org.

www.ingramcontent.com/pod-product-compliance
Lightning Source LLC
Chambersburg PA
CBHW072011290426
44109CB00018B/2205